TEXT AND PSYCHE

TEXT & Psyche

EXPERIENCING SCRIPTURE TODAY

Schuyler Brown

CONTINUUM • NEW YORK

1998
The Continuum Publishing Company
370 Lexington Avenue
New York, NY 10017

Printed in the United States of America

Library of Congress Cataloging-in-Publication Data

Brown, Schuyler.
    Text and psyche : experiencing Scripture today / Schuyler
Brown
        p.   cm.
    Includes bibliographical references.
    ISBN 0-8264-1111-8   (alk. paper)
    1. Bible–Hermeneutics. 2. Bible–Psychology. I. Title.
BS476.B714   1998
220.6`01–dc21
                                                    98-23406
                                                    CIP

Contents 🝢

Nor mouth had, no nor mind, expressed
What heart heard of, ghost guessed

– G<small>ERARD</small> M<small>ANLEY</small> H<small>OPKINS</small>

ACKNOWLEDGMENTS

FIRST OF ALL, I wish to thank Justus George Lawler, without whose enthusiastic interest and encouragement this book might never have seen the light of day. I am also grateful to Michael Fahey, S.J., who, as Dean of the Faculty of Theology of St. Michael's College, granted me a research leave for the purpose of writing this book.

I have presented portions of this manuscript at the Quest for Transformation series, held at Trinity Church, Colborne, Ontario; at the Northrop Frye Symposium, held in Toronto; and at a Bible workshop at the Church of St. Augustine of Canterbury in Toronto. I wish to thank the three individuals who invited me to make these presentations: Graham Cotter, Patrick Johnson, and John Hill.

I am grateful to the C. G. Jung Institute in Zurich for inviting me to lecture on "Text and Psyche."

Finally, I wish to thank Patricia Fleck for assisting me in the preparation of the manuscript and my wife, Margaret Meredith, for her encouragement and advice.

SCHUYLER BROWN
JANUARY 1998

Reading the Bible in a Changed World

When I was a child, I spoke like a child, I thought like a child, I reasoned like a child; when I became a man, I gave up childish ways.
—1 Cor. 13:11

WHEN I WAS growing up in New York City in the 1930s and 1940s, the truth of the Bible was simply not an issue. The Bible was, as a dear relative of mine was wont to remind me, "the word of God, from cover to cover." The fact that the truth of the Bible has *become* an issue reflects far-reaching changes extending over half a century. None of these changes is purely personal to me. I would expect anyone who would read this book to be aware of them and, to one degree or another, to have been affected by them. Therefore, even if your reaction to these changes has been quite different from mine, I hope that by accompanying me on this journey, your *own* reflection on "reading the Bible in a changed world" may be stimulated and enhanced.

"OTHER RELIGIONS" AND THE TRUTH OF THE BIBLE

THE FIRST CHANGE affecting how people view "the truth of the Bible" is the discovery of "other religions." Back in the 1950s, Will Herberg's analysis of "American religion" in terms of "Protestant,

Catholic, and Jew" was still possible.[1] We Christians spoke readily of our "Judeo–Christian" heritage. (Jews never much liked the term, but we rarely took note of this.) The Bible—whether or not this was to include the New Testament could be left a bit vague—was the basis for our understanding of ourselves as a nation and a society.

Today all that has changed.[2] In any large North American city one will find representatives of practically all the "developed" religions of the world. Does "the truth of the Bible" imply that all other religions and their scriptures are false, or that they are true only to the extent that they teach what the Bible teaches? Even a passing acquaintance with "other religions" makes us realize that they often differ so radically from Christianity and Judaism in their assumptions and ways of thinking that any direct comparison is extremely difficult. Each religion articulates the world in its own way.

Moreover, the "religious" group which is expanding most rapidly today is one which scarcely existed when I was growing up: those with no religious affiliation whatever.

Once the theological explanations of "invincible ignorance" and "anonymous Christianity" had lost all plausibility, the pluralism and complexity of the religious phenomenon came to be regarded as a reality to be accepted, rather than as a problem to be explained. We do not expect all people to speak a common language. Why should we expect them to embrace a common religion or a common scripture? But where does this admission leave "the truth of the Bible"?

---

1. Will Herberg, *Protestant–Catholic–Jew* (Garden City, N.Y.: Doubleday, 1956). Herberg criticizes the ambiguous liaison between the three historic faiths and Americanism. He insists that to make religion a mere means to the achievement of temporal prosperity, peace of soul, and the success of Americanism is a sin of idolatry that marks a definitive rejection of the transcendent deity presupposed by each of the three religious traditions.

2. Perhaps an exception should be made for certain parts of the American "Bible Belt."

"THE TRUTH OF THE BIBLE" AND VERIFIABILITY

THE SECOND CHANGE arises out of factors already at work in "Judeo–Christian America," factors which go all the way back to the industrial revolution and even earlier:[3] the influence of technology on the way we think. Our view of "the truth of the Bible" cannot be unaffected by our understanding of truth itself.

Philosophical empiricism, especially Immanuel Kant's critique of metaphysics, called into question the truth of statements not based on sensory data. As Ludwig Wittgenstein's continuation of this critique makes clear, it is based not on accidental or capricious philosophical assumptions but on a religious picture of the world.[4]

In "Judeo–Christian" America religious truths might still have seemed guaranteed by the collective consensus of society. Today, however, truth is coupled in the minds of many people with verifiability. If someone makes an assertion, our first reaction is to ask: what is the evidence for what you say?

In every society there are *values* which enjoy general respect. That is to say, there are certain objects and actions which have social significance. But when religious beliefs are put forward, without evidence, as *facts* demanding universal acceptance, we are clearly dealing with an ideology.[5] Today people are less inclined than they were a generation ago to accept someone else's solution to the problem of human existence, especially when it is presented as collectively obligatory.

---

3. Hans Frei cites the Deist Anthony Collins (1676–1729) as a forerunner of the position of logical positivism that "the meaning of a statement is the method of its verification." (*The Eclipse of Biblical Narrative* [New Haven: Yale University Press, 1974], 77.)

4. Cf. Fergus Kerr, *Theology after Wittgenstein* (Oxford: Blackwell, 1986), chap. 2: "Wittgenstein's Religious Point of View."

5. In *Lectures on Ideology and Utopia* (New York: Columbia University Press, 1986), Paul Ricoeur defines ideology as a mode of the social imagination which projects the community's vision of its own organized reality. It maps out the "constitution" by which the community wishes to identify itself as a social reality.

Now there really *can* be no evidence for religious beliefs, which have to do with "things not seen" (Heb. 11:1; cf. John 20:29). If the "evidence" offered is simply "it's in the Bible" or "that is what the church teaches," then the problem of verifiability is simply pushed back one step further. The ultimate guarantee of religious truth can only be God.

"THE TRUTH OF THE BIBLE" AND THE HISTORICO-CRITICAL METHOD

A THIRD CHANGE affecting "the truth of the Bible" has been the growing prominence of historical criticism. This development has brought no resolution of the challenge posed by "other religions" and scientific technology. For the purpose of historical criticism is not to determine whether or not what the Bible says is true but simply to determine what the Biblical authors *intended* in the context of the world in which they lived.[6] Whether or not we can or should accept what they said as true is simply beside the point. When a distinguished professor and priest was once asked by a student what difference the Old Testament's status as the word of God made for its interpretation, he replied unhesitatingly, "None whatever!"[7]

History, in the usual understanding of the term, is concerned with reconstructing past events which are causally interconnected. In historical criticism of the Bible, however, the emphasis is more on "inner history" than "outer history." By focusing on "the intention of the author" the exegete hopes to reconstruct a "tradition history" or history of ideas. The emphasis on "inner history" is particularly strong in New Testament exegesis.

This sidestepping of the truth question has now come back to haunt us. Surely it must be addressed, but how? I have the impression that historical criticism has had very little impact

---

6. Baruch Spinoza (1632–77) is frequently credited with being the first person to make a distinction between the world as depicted in the Bible and the so-called real world.

7. Sandra Schneiders, *The Revelatory Text* (San Franciso: Harper SanFrancisco, 1991), 2.

among the rank and file of churchgoers. Outside of an academic context, I have rarely heard a sermon which showed much awareness of critical questions affecting the interpretation of scripture. Now to ignore an approach to the Bible which has produced such notable results reminds me of those believers in Ptolemaic astronomy who refused to look through Galileo's telescope. On the other hand, I must acknowledge that historical criticism is more *informative* than *transformative,* and what religious people are usually looking for when they turn to the Bible is truth and personal transformation.

THE HISTORICAL PARADIGM

IF HISTORICAL CRITICISM is unable to contribute to either of these objectives, it has, at least, made certain ways of reading the Bible problematical. The two basic paradigms for reading the Bible, prior to the advent of historical criticism, were history and doctrine. Indeed, in the Middle Ages the very understanding of history was derived from the Bible. History was the sequence of saving events revealed in the sacred text and extending from Genesis to Revelation.

Most of the controversy about the Bible involves the understanding of "history." "*Sacred* history," derived from the literary sequence of the biblical books, now has to compete with an understanding of history as a scholarly reconstruction of the past based on the critical evaluation and interpretation of sources.[8]

The question whether and to what extent the Bible is "historically true" is really beside the point. The point is rather whether "history"—understood as referring to past events or simply to the "intention" of the author[9]—can still serve as an appropriate paradigm for "the truth of the Bible." In the modern understanding of history, scholarly inquiry can only arrive at probability, which means, concretely, what the scholar's colleagues in the field are more or less prepared to accept. Historical reconstruction never

---

8. Cf. E. H. Carr, *What Is History?* (New York City: Penguin Books, 1978).

9. Frei refers to this post-Enlightenment approach to the biblical text as "meaning as ostensive or ideal reference" (*Eclipse of Biblical Narrative, passim*).

attains the certitude which faith requires, and it is obliged to subject *all* sources to critical scrutiny. Canonical status is no guarantee of historical reliability.

In these circumstances, to continue to talk about "salvation history" as a record of the past which is immune to critical questioning can only generate confusion. In my opinion, "the truth of the Bible" simply cannot be understood to be "what actually happened" (in Leopold von Ranke's famous phrase), as reported in the biblical text.

The futility of seeking saving faith in the probabilities of history is well expressed by the Protestant mystic, Angelus Silesius:

> *If Christ is born a thousand times in Bethlehem, but not in*
> *thee, thou art still eternally lost.*
> *The cross on Golgotha cannot redeem thee from evil,*
> *if it is not erected in thy heart.*
> *I tell thee, it is no help to thee that Christ is risen,*
> *if thou still liest in sin and the bonds of death.*[10]

THE DOCTRINAL PARADIGM

AN EMINENT NEW TESTAMENT scholar, who is also a popular preacher, once confided to me that he would rather preach on Paul than on the Gospels, since this avoided having to deal with "historical problems." Now it is true that doctrinal affirmations do not carry the same risk of being proven false as affirmations concerning the occurrence of past events. But is the doctrinal paradigm really any less of a problem for understanding "the truth of the Bible"? If we do not limit ourselves to Paul, as a "canon within the canon," but consider the doctrine proposed in *all* the New Testament writings, then we find a doctrinal diversity which contrasts with the relative uniformity of the early creeds.

The early church writer Tertullian was keenly aware of the problems which could be generated by searching the scripture. He writes:

---

10. Angelus Silesius, *Cherubinischer Wandersmann* (Breslau, 1675), I, 61–63 (my translation).

> There is one definite truth taught by Christ which the nations
> are bound by every means to believe, and therefore to seek, so
> that when they have found it they may believe it. Thou must
> seek until thou findest, and thou must believe when thou hast
> found. And then nothing more remains for thee to do, save to
> keep what thou hast believed.[11]

Historical criticism has made it difficult, if not impossible, to follow Tertullian's advice. For we are now obliged to recognize that the apparent simplicity of the "rule of faith" conceals the doctrinal diversity of scripture itself. For example, the Nicene–Constantinopolitan Creed, in confessing that Jesus Christ is "the only Son of God, eternally begotten of the Father," depends on the Johannine prologue, where Christ is called "the Father's only Son" (John 1:14) and is identified with the Word, which "was in the beginning with God and was God" (1:1). But when that same Creed goes on to say that Christ "was born of the Virgin Mary by the power of the Spirit," it is dependent on the Matthean and Lucan infancy narratives, both of which explain Jesus' premature conception by the influence of the Spirit of God (Matt. 1:18–25; Luke 1:26–38). The Creed has conflated John's pre-existence Christology, according to which Christ was God's Son before the world was created, with Luke's conception Christology, which declares Jesus to be God's Son because of the intervention of the Spirit at his conception (Luke 1:35).

Before I had ever heard of deconstruction, I was exposed to its approach through historical criticism. The consistency and uniformity which are required in doctrinal formulations are undermined by the disclosure of the underlying diversity and pluralism of the scriptural bases for these formulations.[12] If "the truth of the Bible" cannot be understood as "what actually happened," neither can it be understood to be "what really is," if this is taken to mean a world of self-consistent and unchanging realities beyond the range of human experience.

---

11. Tertullian, *On the "Prescription" of Heretics* (trans. T. H. Bindley; London: SPCK, 1914), 49.

12. It does not seem to me that G. A. Lindbeck's "postliberal" rehabilitation of doctrine (*The Nature of Doctrine* [Philadelphia: Westminster Press, 1984]) gives sufficient attention to this problem.

Indeed, it is only when Christian doctrine is seen in a relationship of living reciprocity to the psyche, from which it originated, that the appearance of "sacrosanct unintelligibility" can be avoided.[13] The contradictions which arise when doctrinal formulations are subjected to critical analysis lead us to an appreciation of their proper function: to give symbolic expression to a transcendent fact that cannot be explained rationally.[14] Blind obedience to church dogma, without an experience of its living relationship to the psyche, leads to the despair which Jung observed in his pastor father.[15]

The doctrinal diversity which I have just illustrated in Christology is even more apparent in ethics. Although the Bible has a great deal to say about sin, it does not have a coherent *doctrine* of sin. Its message does not include an unambiguous identification of evil; rather, it reflects the shifting experience of evil throughout biblical history.[16]

"THE TRUTH OF THE BIBLE" AND RATIONAL ANALYSIS

HOWEVER MUCH HISTORICAL and doctrinal approaches to the Bible may differ, they are at one in their use of rational categories to analyze the sacred text. The systematic *con*struction of doctrine by the theologian and the critical *re*construction of the past by the historical critic have much in common. Now the Bible, like any other text, can be subjected to conceptual explication. But as Jung has observed, "the spirit does not dwell in concepts."[17] There is a tension between the religious phenomenon which is mediated by the biblical text and the rational analysis of this phenomenon. "Explaining" religion can easily become "explaining it away."

---

13. C. G. Jung, *Collected Works* (henceforth "*CW*") (Princeton, N.J.: Princeton University Press), vol. 11, 109, 111.

14. Jung, *CW*, vol. 11, 140. Jung reminds us here that the Latin word for *creed* is appropriately *symbolum*.

15. C. G. Jung, *Memories, Dreams, Reflections,* ed. Aniela Jaffé, trans. Richard and Clara Winston (Glasgow: Fount, 1977), 112–16.

16. Schuyler Brown, "Sin and Atonement: Biblical Imagery and the Experience of Evil," *Union Seminary Quarterly Review* 44 (1990), 150–56.

17. Jung, *Memories, Dreams, Reflections,* 167.

Our religious instinct and our reasoning faculty seem to be located in different parts of the brain. Even in physics, the Heisenberg principle tells us, a phenomenon is not unaffected by its being observed. The rational analysis of a religious text may be compared with the entomologist's study of a butterfly: it can kill the living reality which is being examined.

Historical criticism is the child of the eighteenth-century Enlightenment, and the rationalism which is inherent in it is often taken to be inimical to faith. It has, however, performed an invaluable service by showing what faith is *not* and by unmasking the rationalism which often parades in faith's place.

These, then, are three important factors which have changed our world, as far as reading the Bible is concerned. Daily contacts with those of "other religions" and no religion make it difficult to understand "the truth of the Bible" to mean a collection of "facts" put forward for universal acceptance under pain of eternal sanctions. The relation between truth and verifiability in modern technological society, especially in an academic environment, makes one query the meaning of a "truth" whose guarantor can only be God. Finally, exposure to the historico-critical method has made it difficult to understand "the truth of the Bible" in terms of either of the two predominant paradigms: history and doctrine.[18] The truth of the Bible, it would seem, refers neither to something "back then" nor to something "out there." It pertains to another realm altogether, the realm of the spirit, the world which is evoked so powerfully by the archaic imagery of Byzantine iconography.[19]

"THE TRUTH OF THE BIBLE" AND LIBERATION

TO THESE THREE factors should be added, at least in passing, other experiences which influence modern men and women as they

---

18. The difficulty that people have in understanding the truth of the Bible on any other terms than "what really happened" is evident both in the approach taken by the Jesus Seminar and in the vehement reactions to its "findings."

19. *Anglican–Orthodox Dialogue: The Dublin Agreed Statement 1984* (Crestwood, N.Y.: St. Vladimir's Seminary Press, 1985), 40: "An icon . . . guides us to a vision of the divine Kingdom where past, present and future are one."

read the Bible. I am thinking of such things as personal tragedy and loss, the experience of poverty and economic oppression, the injustice of racial and sexual discrimination, the dark presence in our world of war, genocide, and tyranny. For those living under the shadow of such experiences, the Bible must convey some response to their plight, if it is to be considered the word of God.

IS THE MEANING OF THE BIBLE "OBJECTIVELY" DETERMINED?

NOW THERE ARE those both in the Church and in the academy who would vigorously contest the starting-point of this chapter, namely, the view that all interpretation is affected by the particular circumstances of the interpreter. For such persons the meaning of the Bible is eternally fixed in the mind of God and/or the human author, and the purpose of interpretation is to recover this original meaning. This is not the place to debate this issue. I would simply observe that in the history of biblical interpretation text and personal experience have not usually been "two autonomous domains. On the contrary, they are reciprocally enlightening: even as the immediate event helps make the age-old text intelligible, so in turn the text reveals the fundamental significance of the recent event or experience."[20]

Perhaps the most celebrated illustration of this generalization is Matthew's interpretation of Isa. 7:14 (Matt. 1:23). The Evangelist shows no interest in what this prophecy might have meant in the immediate context of the reign of King Ahaz. He unhesitatingly interprets it in terms of his own Christian faith (Matt. 1:18–22). The Bible, like any literary work, has a life in history, and the shifting perceptions of its meaning, as it is passed on from age to age, are as much a part of it as the meaning intended by the original author or perceived by the original audience.[21]

---

20. Judah Goldin, in Shalom Spiegel, *The Last Trial* (New York: Pantheon Books, 1967), xvi.

21. This point is acknowledged in the *Evangelisch-Katholischer Kommentar* ("Protestant–Catholic Commentary") series, by the inclusion of sections on "*Wirkungsgeschichte*," i.e., the history of the *effect* that scripture has had down through the centuries.

For all that we have learned from historical criticism, we must acknowledge its principal shortcoming: by isolating a text in its own age and situation of origin, it prevents it from saying something to the present,[22] and that is precisely what scripture is expected to do.[23] By distancing the reader from the text, historical criticism runs the risk of frustrating the immediacy which is characteristic of religious literature. Instead of being summoned to question and deepen the way in which we view ourselves and the world, we are allowed and even encouraged, to take a detached, "objective" point of view: we analyze what the author intended to communicate to the original readers; we ourselves do not stand within the hermeneutical circle.

THE NARRATIVE PARADIGM

MY INTEREST IN literary criticism of the Bible was occasioned by this problem. The literary approach does allow more scope for theoretical questions, of the sort addressed by hermeneutics, than is possible within historical criticism,[24] and these questions will be the subject of a later chapter. However, literary criticism does not, in itself, provide a solution to the problem of retrieving "the truth of the Bible."

In particular, we need to consider how the Bible *as narrative* relates to the problem of its truth. Frank Kermode has reminded us that narratives are intrinsically obscure,[25] and they can also be seductive and manipulative. Although many people today approach biblical narrative with deep suspicions, which are not

22. Ulrich Luz, *Das Evangelium nach Matthäus* (Zurich: Benziger, 1985), vol. l, 79.

23. See Peter Williamson, "Actualization: A New Emphasis in Catholic Scripture Study," *America,* May 20, 1995, 17–19, and Joseph Fitzmyer's critical response (*America,* June 17, 1995, 37–38).

24. Frei (*Eclipse of Biblical Narrative,* 56) declares: "The relation between historical citicism and hermeneutics has remained an unresolved issue ever since its inception in the eighteenth century."

25. Frank Kermode, *The Genesis of Secrecy: On the Interpretation of Narrative* (Cambridge: Harvard University Press, 1979), chap. 2: "Hoti's Business: Why Are Narratives Obscure?"

limited to the question of historical verifiability, it nevertheless continues to exercise a mysterious power of attraction.

I do not think it feasible, in our present situation, to try to reverse the split between biblical narrative and history by declaring the former to be beyond all human judgment or critique. Most scriptures of the world make such "an imperialistic claim,"[26] and there can be no obvious reason for privileging one of them. If the advent of historical criticism has really meant "the death of scripture,"[27] a rebirth would require not another theological affirmation of scripture's special status but a renewed experience of its power.

Hans Frei observes,

> The Bible was for the older Protestants a coherent world of discourse in its own right, whose depictions and teachings had a reality of their own, though to be sure, it was the reality into which all men had to fit, and in one way or another did fit.[28]

The loss of this sense of being contained within the biblical narrative has had portentous consequences, like the loss of innocence in the Garden of Eden. However, it marks a stage in the development of human consciousness which cannot be reversed.

BIBLICAL NARRATIVE AND MODERN FICTION

MUCH OF THE recent study of narrative by biblical scholars has focused on the eighteenth- and nineteenth-century English novel. The fact that the application of "narrative criticism" to the Bible is technically possible does not guarantee that it will prove illuminating. Certain key distinctions used in modern narrative criticism, such as the distinction between "implied author" and "narrator," have no application in Gospel narrative, and this should give us pause: is this model appropriate? I have the impression

---

26. G. W. Stroup, *The Promise of Narrative Theology* (Atlanta, Ga.: Knox, 1981), 81.

27. Robert Morgan with John Barton, *Biblical Interpretation* (Oxford University Press, 1988), chap. 2: "Criticism and the Death of Scripture."

28. Frei, *Eclipse of Biblical Narrative*, 90.

that the narrative paradigm has sometimes been used as a way of evading tough historical questions and of introducing doctrinal assumptions in narrative disguise.

The Bible is *neither* history *nor* literature, in the modern acceptation of these terms. This has been brought home to me by a recent literary analysis of the Fourth Gospel,[29] which, I must confess, I found ultimately disappointing. For if one reads the Fourth Gospel with the expectations normally attached to modern fiction, one will be disappointed, despite individual passages of great narrative power (e.g., John 9:1–41, 18:28–38). If the work is taken as a whole, neither the story nor the characters make any claim to realism. There is no pretense at dramatic tension; the outcome of the story is known from the beginning: "he came unto his own, and his own received him not" (John 1:11).

The baffling breaks and discontinuities in the story are symptomatic of a broader problem: the episodic character of the narrative as a whole. Hardly any of the characters have a life of their own. Jesus, the Beloved Disciple, and John the Baptist are simply projections of the narrator: his voice speaks through them all, with no discernible difference in style or content.

The "heavies" in the drama are shallow and superficially drawn. No knowledge is given to the reader of what actually makes them tick. They are simply stand-ins for the world, the flesh, and the devil. In fact, the disappointing narrative is but a thin veil cast over a work of religious propaganda.[30]

In reading a novel, "one temporarily takes leave of one's familiar world of reality and enters into another world that is autonomous in its own right."[31] But is such a "willing suspension of disbelief" really possible in the case of the Gospels?

Of course, modern novelists may also have propagandistic objectives, but, to be effective, they must move the reader by the

---

29. R. A. Culpepper, *Anatomy of the Fourth Gospel* (Philadelphia: Fortress, 1983).

30. Cf. Hans Frei, *Eclipse of Biblical Narrative*, 12: "written forms of self-committing statements which make sense by evoking similar dispositions on the part of the reader."

31. J. D. Kingsbury, *Matthew as Story* (Philadelphia: Fortress, 1986), 2.

way they tell their story. That is why one may become thoroughly engrossed in a Charles Dickens novel, for example, even
though the particular social evils against which he was writing are
a thing of the past.

To be sure, many biblical narratives *do* move the reader by the
way they tell their story, and this may be the effect of their being
what Frei calls "history-like"[32]—a characteristic which has surely
received insufficient attention in historical criticism. However,
this need not lead us to the Barthian move of declaring biblical
narrative beyond all human criticism, nor is biblical narrative's
"history-like" quality necessarily clarified by a comparison with
the English novel. What Denis de Rougemont says about the difference between art and myth could equally well be said of the
difference between the modern novel and biblical narrative:

> The validity of a work of art depends on nothing but the talent of
> its author. . . . *But the most profound characteristic of a myth is the
> power which it wins over us, usually without our knowing.*[33]

THE TRUTH OF THE PARABLE

ONE WAY TO approach the problem of "the truth of the Bible" would
be to start with the type of narrative which Jesus seems to have
favored: the parable. According to C. H. Dodd's famous definition,

> the parable is a metaphor or simile drawn from nature or com-
> mon life, arresting the hearer by its vividness or strangeness,
> and leaving the mind in sufficient doubt about its precise appli-
> cation to tease it into active thought.[34]

The parable, as an "extended metaphor," uses the secular
everyday language of human experience, but it cracks the surface
realism in order to give us a glimpse of something lying beyond
it. As though through a screen or grid, we see something new and

---

32. Hans Frei, *Eclipse of Biblical Narrative*, 1–16.
33. Denis de Rougemont, *Love in the Western World*, trans.
Montgomery Belgion (Princeton, N.J.: Princeton University Press, 1983), 19.
34. C. H. Dodd, *The Parables of the Kingdom* (New York: Scribner's,
1961), 5.

extraordinary which is not the direct object of affirmation at all. The parable is a vehicle of insight, which leads to action.[35]

Unlike the most famous Old Testament parable, which the prophet Nathan delivers to King David (2 Sam. 12:1–4), the parables of Jesus rely upon the intuition of the hearer to find a personal significance. Jesus does not declare, "You are the man" (2 Sam. 12:7), but rather, "He that has ears to hear, let him hear" (Mark 4:9). Although Gospel commentators have not hesitated to tell us what they think the parables mean, whether in the historical context of Jesus' ministry or in the literary context of the Gospels, the form itself resists this procedure. For if a parable could be reduced to a single meaning, the parable itself would be superfluous. Rather, the parable provides a paradigm for the uniquely personal way in which a powerful image can lead to insight and transformation.

RESOURCES FOR RETRIEVING "THE TRUTH OF THE BIBLE"

THE PAST FIFTY years have challenged our naive, uncritical understanding of the truth of the Bible, but they have also brought resources for meeting this challenge and for retrieving a belief in the Bible as the word of God. For some—myself included—a major resource has been the Anglican tradition. Anglicanism is an anomaly in the spectrum of Christian denominationalism: a nonconfessional church. Not only does it have no *magisterium* or teaching authority; it possesses no confessional declarations comparable to the Augsburg Confession for Lutherans or the Westminster Confession for Presbyterians.[36] *The Book of Common Prayer* retained the ancient Christian creeds, but even they are subject to the proviso that "Holy Scripture containeth all things necessary to salvation" (Sixth Article of Religion).

The English Reformation differed from the Reformation on the continent: the Church of England was confronted with the task of

---

35. Sallie McFague, *Speaking in Parables* (Philadelphia: Fortress, 1975).

36. The XXXIX Articles have never enjoyed the same status in Anglicanism as the historic Reformation confessions, and today they are rarely referred to.

serving the interests of national unity by bringing together as many Christians as possible within the unity of a single state church. Thus the Church of England came to include both the followers of continental Protestantism, especially in its Calvinist form, and those who remained attached to the pre-Reformation church. Consequently, the English Reformation was not so much a doctrinal as a *liturgical* reformation.[37] Its principal architect, Thomas Cranmer, had the task of turning scripture into liturgy, or, to put it another way, of devising a liturgy of which scripture would be the inspiration and *raison d'être.*

Cranmer believed that the Bible, as the living word of God, comes with the greatest power when unaccompanied by any human gloss, comment, or exposition. Consequently, in the Anglican tradition, the minister of the Word is primarily the person authorized to *read* the word of God in the congregation.[38] Anglicanism's emphasis on *texts* rather than doctrine forms a link between the twelfth-century concept of *lectio divina* (spiritual reading) and modern literary theory. The iconoclasm of the English Reformation did away with painted images, but it preserved the verbal icon in the auditory images of the English Bible and its liturgical transposition, *The Book of Common Prayer.*

TEXT AND PSYCHE

ANOTHER RESOURCE FOR retrieving the truth of the Bible is the work of Jung, who has made the claim: "We must read our Bible or we shall not understand psychology."[39] As a pastor's son, he was deeply versed in sacred scripture and also quite familiar with the methods—and limitations—of contemporary historical exegesis.[40] Although skeptical of doctrinal truth claims, Jung acknowledged,

---

37. Cf. J. N. Wall, *Transformations of the Word* (Athens and London: University of Georgia Press, 1988), "Prologue: Poetry and Reformation in Renaissance England."

38. Stephen Neill, *Anglicanism* (New York: Oxford University Press, 1977), 54–55.

39. C. G. Jung, *The Visions Seminars* (Zurich: Spring Publications, 1976), vol. 1, 156.

40. See Wayne Rollins, *Jung and the Bible* (Atlanta, Ga.: Knox, 1983).

as a physician, the therapeutic benefits of religious faith, and he regarded the absence of a religious attitude as the root of much contemporary neurosis.

I believe that the converse of Jung's dictum is also true: without psychology it is difficult to understand the Bible or the truth claims which are made on its behalf. If the Bible's claim to truth rests neither on its being a history book nor on its being a manual of doctrine, then perhaps we should seek the basis for such a claim in the uncanny power of the sacred text to transform human lives.[41] The transformative experience which Bible reading engenders is a work of divine grace, but if we ask *where* this work takes place, the answer can only be: in the human soul.

"Soul" is out of fashion in contemporary theology, since it is regarded as an unbiblical import from Greek anthropology. However, in Jung's way of thinking, *psyche* (the Greek word for "soul") is not a metaphysical substance; rather, it refers to the process out of which *all* a person's spiritual acts emerge. During the second millennium of the Christian era a myth of rationality has taken hold which excludes the soul, just as it excludes the divine. Modern men and women have lost the vision of transcendence and have traded the soul's values for the rational intellect's instrumental powers.[42] In contemporary discourse the use of the term "soul" is therefore unavoidable, if the human spirit is not to be limited to the rational functions of thinking and willing.[43]

In the mystical tradition the locus of the divine action is called the "bottom" or "ground" of the soul (*fundus animae*). This deep abyss, which we cannot sound, corresponds to Jung's understanding of the unconscious, which is not a mere storehouse of repressed personal material, as it is in Sigmund Freud, but rather the primal source out of which the ego itself, with its rational

---

41. Cf. Walter Wink, *The Bible in Human Transformation* (Philadelphia: Fortress Press, 1973).

42. Murray Stein, *Jung's Treatment of Christianity* (Wilmette, Ill.: Chiron, 1986), 104.

43. James Hillman has played the leading role in reintroducing "soul" into contemporary psychological discussion. See *The Soul's Code* (New York: Random House, 1996).

powers, emerges. The archaic imagery in which all religions find expression has its source in this *transpersonal* unconscious, by which the imagination of the individual is seeded from childhood on. This blind wisdom or seminal brain, commonly called instinct, seems to sheathe a certain omniscience.[44]

The mysterious transformation effected by reading the Bible cannot be explained, I believe, if the biblical text is taken to be simply what the author has rationally conceived and rhetorically expressed. It must also be understood as the *mimesis* of the psychic processes which produced it. Whatever the author's conscious intention may have been, a religious text arises out of a world of archetypal imagery, and a responsive reader is able to penetrate, through the surface level of the text, to those deep structures which powerfully engage his or her unconscious feelings. The religious function of the Bible is not so much to inform the mind, as it is "to change the blood" (D. H. Lawrence).[45]

The Numinous Text

JUNG WAS GREATLY influenced by Rudolf Otto's work on "the Holy,"[46] a term which originally had nothing to do with the ethical meaning which it commonly has today. "The Holy" is "the utterly other," a numinous reality which provokes a reaction of awe and fascination. Otto believed the origin of religion to lie in this experience of the uncanny. All religions have undergone a process of rationalization and moralization (a process which is amply attested in the Bible), but their root lies in something which is nonrational,

---

44. I am paraphrasing Ralph Waldo Emerson, who is quoted in Gloria L. Young, "The Fountainhead of All Forms" in *Artful Thunder,* ed. R. J. DeMott and S. E. Marovitz (Kent, Ohio: Kent State University Press), 242.

45. Wayne Rollins, "Jung's Challenge to Contemporary Hermeneutics" in *Jung's Challenge to Contemporary Religion,* ed. Murray Stein and R. L. Moore (Wilmette, Ill.: Chiron, 1987), 114. Spinoza expressed the same thought: "its [i.e., scripture's] object is not to convince the reason, but to attract and lay hold of the imagination." (*The Chief Works of Benedict de Spinoza,* trans. R. H. M. Elwes [New York: Dover, 1951], vol. 1, 91.)

46. Rudolf Otto, *The Idea of the Holy,* trans. J. W. Harvey (Oxford University Press, 1958).

a primal experience which engages the emotions rather than the intellect and which need not receive any verbal expression.

There are many reflections of this sort of experience in the Bible. Jacob reacts to his vision at Bethel with the words: "How awesome is this place!" (Gen. 28:17), and after his wrestling match by the Jabbok river (Gen. 32:24), he vainly asks his mysterious adversary to tell him his name (v. 29). Moses sees a bush that burns with fire but is not consumed (Exod. 3:2), and he is assaulted by the Lord with deadly intent (Exod 4:24). The Lord answers Job out of the whirlwind (Job 38:1), and the righteous hero's reaction is one of self-abhorrence and repentance (Job 42:6). In the New Testament Jesus provokes a similar response, both during his life (Luke 5:8; 7:6 par) and after his death (Luke 24:37).

Otto is not alone in this explanation of the origin of religion. In *The Varieties of Religious Experience,* William James declares: "Instinct leads, intelligence does but follow."[47] If feelings and instinct are at the heart of the religious experience, then we would expect these elements to have an importance in both the production and the reception of religious texts. The experience of the Holy does not, of course, depend upon a written scripture, but in religions which *have* a scripture, one would expect it to serve as a catalyst for such experiences, and such, in fact, is the case. A colleague of mine whose field is the Hebrew Bible remarked at a recent conference: "The Bible is a horrible book, but I love the old monster!"

"LET THE READER UNDERSTAND!" (MARK 13:14)

IN BOTH HISTORICAL and doctrinal interpretation, the intention of the author (human or divine) permits a text to have but one correct meaning. (Of course, double meanings, such as we find in the Fourth Gospel, may both have been intended by the author.) In modern literary theory, however, diversity of interpretation is taken for granted, and this has important consequences for evaluating the history of biblical interpretation.

---

47. William James, *The Varieties of Religious Experience* (London: Fontana, 1975), 88.

Jung considered the Gnostics to be theologians who allowed themselves to be influenced in large measure by inner experience, as is amply attested by the Gnostic interpretation of biblical texts. From a modern exegetical standpoint, the Gnostic reading of Genesis is bizarre and even perverse, but this, I believe, is because the Gnostics picked up aspects of the text which orthodox theologians ignored. The symbolic language of the Genesis story fired the imagination of the Gnostic interpreter, so that Gnostic literature can be called "a veritable mine of information concerning all those natural symbols arising out of the repercussions of the Christian message."[48]

In the twelfth century, the monastic practice of *lectio divina* was motivated by the same search for holy wisdom which had inspired the Gnostic reader: to expose oneself to the light emanating from the page, so that, in the light of the wisdom that brings the page to glow, the self of the reader will catch fire, and in its light recognize himself.[49]

In modern times the reading process has been secularized. Literacy is the prerequisite for effective citizenship, and reading the Bible is expected to provide either information (for the believer) or *dis*information (for the skeptic). By contrast, for the Gnostic and the monk the text was an oracle, and reading was an act of divination.

THE TRUTH OF THE BIBLE

AN APPROACH TO the Bible as a numinous text rather than as a source of information can lead to a retrieval of its truth—not the truth of ancient fact or inerrant doctrine but truth in the etymological sense of the Greek word used by the New Testament writers: *aletheia.*

The underlying verb, which means "to escape notice," is combined here with the negative prefix, suggesting the meaning: "no longer hidden." The philosopher Martin Heidegger used this etymology in his understanding of truth as "coming into the open": a

---

48. Jung, *CW,* vol. 9, pt. 2, 269.
49. Cf. Ivan Illich, *In the Vineyard of the Text* (Chicago: University of Chicago Press, 1993), 17.

process through which the world comes into being in the light of human consciousness. The etymology also suggests another Greek word: *photismos,* "illumination" or "enlightenment."[50] In the light of the Bible's numinous radiance the world is no longer "a cheerless clockwork fantasy [where] there is no drama of man, world, and God . . . but only the dreariness of calculated processes."[51]

The Bible is true, on this understanding, not because its content is verifiable, but because reading the Bible enlightens the reader. As the Psalmist writes, "Thy word is a lamp to my feet and a light to my path" (Ps. 119:105). As Jews and Christians have always known, reading the Bible illumines our path, so that we can live our lives with hope and integrity. Reading the Bible in a changed world can still change our world and fill it with meaning and purpose.

This understanding of the truth of the Bible is not exclusivist. On the contrary, when truth is understood in this way, it serves to connect the Bible with other sacred texts, which, whatever the difference in doctrine or beliefs, have the same function: to make available to the concious mind, through thte use of symbolic imagery, the transformative energy of the affections.[52]

---

50. See Graeme Nicholson, *Seeing and Reading* (London: Macmillan, 1984), chap. 4, "Illumination."

51. Jung, *Memories, Dreams, Reflections,* 284.

52. Schuyler Brown, "The True Light," *Toronto Journal of Theology* 1/2 (Fall 1985), 222–26.

1. Biblical Empirics

Did not our hearts burn within us . . .
while he opened to us the scriptures?
—Luke 24:32

THE MYSTICAL THEOLOGIAN who lived c. 500 and is known to history as Pseudo-Dionysius[53] writes of one of his teachers that "he not only learned (*mathôn*) divine things but also experienced/suffered (*pathôn*) them."[54] The theme of "knowledge through experience/suffering/passion"[55] pervades Western literature from Aeschylus[56] to the Tristan and Iseult legend.[57] The author of the Letter to the Hebrews says of Christ that "he learned through what he suffered" (Heb. 5:8). The knowledge in question is not abstract or theoretical but personal and existential. The words of the Emmaus

---

53. Also known as "the Pseudo-Areopagite," this writer was identified until the sixteenth century with Paul's convert at Athens (Acts 17:34). The supposed apostolic authority of his writings, added to their intrinsic value, caused them to exercise a profound influence on medieval theology both in the East and in the West.

54. Pseudo-Dionysius, *The Divine Names,* 2.9. See Paul Rorem, *Pseudo-Dionysius* (New York: Oxford University Press, 1993), 143. There is a Greek pun on the words "learn" and "experience."

55. All three meanings are included in the Greek verb, as well as in the Latin verb, from which "passion" is derived.

56. Aeschylus, *Agamemnon,* v. 177.

57. de Rougemont, *Love in the Western World,* 51: "Both passion and the longing for death which passion disguises are connected with, and fostered by, a particular notion of how to reach understanding which in itself is typical of the Western *psyche.* Why does Western Man wish to suffer this passion which lacerates him and which all his common sense rejects? . . . The answer is that he reaches self-awareness and tests himself only by risking his life—in suffering and on the verge of death."

disciples quoted above bear witness to scripture's role as the catalyst in this mysterious process: in the "chance" encounter between
the disciples and the risen Lord, the scripture mediates a new
insight into who Jesus is and why he had to suffer.

This experiential dimension of Bible reading is amply attested
within the Bible itself. The Psalmist proclaims the blessedness of
those whose "delight is in the law of the Lord" (Ps. 1:2). The ordi-
nances of the Lord are "sweeter than honey and drippings of the
honeycomb" (Ps. 19:10). When Ezekiel was given the scroll to eat,
he declared that "it was in my mouth as sweet as honey" (Ezek. 3:3;
cf. Rev. 10:9). Paul declares that the Bible was written "that by the
encouragement of the scriptures we might have hope" (Rom. 15:4).

Similar testimony is found throughout the history of the
Christian church. John Henry Newman writes at the beginning of
his *Apologia*: "I was brought up from a child to take great delight in
reading the Bible. . . ."[58] A hymn stanza asks rhetorically:

> *Who can tell the pleasure*
> *Who recount the treasure*
> *By thy Word imparted*
> *To the simple-hearted?*[59]

John Wesley writes:

> In the evening [of May 24], I went very unwillingly to a soci-
> ety in Aldersgate Street, where one was reading Luther's
> Preface to the Epistle to the Romans. About a quarter before
> nine, while he was describing the change which God works in
> the heart through faith in Christ, *I felt my heart strangely warmed*
> [my emphasis].[60]

---

58. John Henry Newman, *Apologia Pro Vita Sua* (London: Sheed
and Ward, 1978), 1. The sentence continues: ". . . but I had no formed
religious convictions till I was fifteen." The child's "delight" in reading
the Bible is contrasted with "formed religious convictions," to the evident disadvantage of the former.

59. The Rev. Sir H. W. Baker (1861) in *The Book of Common Praise*
(Toronto: Oxford University Press, n.d.), 452.

60. *John and Charles Wesley: Selected Papers, Hymns, Journal Notes,
Sermons, Letters, and Treatises,* ed. Frank Whaling (Toronto: Paulist Press,

In this kind of reading, the reader is truly a reader, and not a critic. Such a reader does not stand over against the text, but rather is penetrated by the text, and, through openness and attention, may experience a dynamic passivity which can border on the ecstatic or the transcendent.[61]

A classic example of such a reading of the Bible is found in the eighth book of Augustine's *Confessions*. Weary of his present life, yet unable to come to any decision to change, Augustine responds to a voice which says repeatedly, "Take it and read." He opens a book containing Paul's epistles and reads the first passage on which his eyes fall:

> Not in revelling and drunkenness, not in lust and wantonness, not in quarrels and rivalries. Rather, arm yourselves with the Lord Jesus Christ and spend no more thought on nature and nature's appetites (Rom. 13:13–14).

Augustine continues:

> I had no wish to read more and no need to do so. For in an instant, as I came to the end of the sentence, it was as though the light of confidence flooded into my heart and all the darkness of doubt was dispelled.[62]

Athanasius tells us in his *Life of Saint Antony* that six months after the death of Antony's parents the saint was on his way to church. At the very moment that he entered the building,

> the Gospel was being read, and he heard the passage in which the Lord says to the rich man: *If thou wilt be perfect, go sell all that thou hast, and give it to the poor; and come, follow me and thou shalt have treasure in Heaven* (Matt. 19:21). As though God had put him in mind of the saints and *as though the reading had been directed especially to him,* Antony immediately left the church and gave to the townspeople the property he had from his forebears.[63]

---

61. Cf. George Steiner, "'Critic'/'Reader,'" *New Literary History* 10 (1979) 423–52.

62. Augustine, *Confessions,* trans. R. S. Pine–Coffin (Penguin Books, 1975), 178.

63. Athanasius, *Life of Saint Anthony* (Westminster, Md.: 1950),

In this kind of reading (or hearing) experience, historical distance is transcended and the scriptural word of God is experienced as direct address.

THE PARALLEL WITH LITERATURE

IN THE PASSAGES just cited, "burning hearts," "sweetness," "consolation," "hope," "delight," "pleasure," and "confidence" all refer to present experience. The message received by Augustine and Antony was in the form of a revelation sent directly by God. Similarly, in reading literature the emphasis is on the *present* experience of reading, in which the reader has the impression of being addressed directly by the author. We can enjoy the plays of William Shakespeare without knowing anything about how they came to be written. We do not need to know when or where a play was first performed; we do not even have to be certain of the author's identity. (Were the plays perhaps written, after all, by Edward de Vere, the seventeenth earl of Oxford?) Nor are we especially concerned with the accuracy with which past events are represented. Even if a historical play were shown to be crude Tudor propaganda, its impact on the reader would not necessarily be effected. Whatever Shakespeare's historical intentions may have been, the work is measured against something outside the author.[64]

The status of a text as a work of literature has nothing to do with its origin or even with the "truth" (i.e., verifiability) of its contents; literary status depends solely on the mysterious power of a text to interest and move the reader. Speaking for an ironic age, W. H. Auden declared, "Poetry makes nothing happen."[65] Nevertheless, no one who actually reads literature believes this to be true. An encounter with a work of literature is sought in order to explore the possibilities of existence and to question and deepen the way in which the reader views him- or herself and the

64. See W. K. Wimsatt Jr. and M. C. Beardsley, *The Verbal Icon: Studies in the Meaning of Poetry* (Lexington: University of Kentucky Press, 1954), 3–18.

65. Quoted in Jonathan Culler, *The Pursuit of Signs* (Ithaca, N.Y.: Cornell University Press, 1981), 140.

world.[66] A reader is drawn to a classic literary text not only by the desire for enjoyable diversion but also by an interest in spiritual adventure or in personal and social transformation.[67]

In order to enjoy literature, a "willing suspension of disbelief" may be necessary. If I want to enjoy a novel by Dickens, I cannot simultaneously apply my critical faculties to pointing out the exaggeration in his characterization or the implausibility in his plots. Legitimate as these questions may be, they detract from literary appreciation, for which the reader must enter, freely, into the world of the text. To be genuinely open to any experience, whether in reading or in life, we must be able to defer analysis and evaluation. Reading has been compared to seeing,[68] and in both activities experience precedes reflection.

THE BIBLE AS SCRIPTURE

THE BIBLE, OF course, is not simply literature. The action taken by the synagogue and the church in "canonizing" these particular texts has given them a special status not only within communities of faith but even in the general culture. This scriptural status is not intrinsic to the works themselves: no biblical author thought he or she was writing scripture. But the scriptural status which these texts have acquired has a definite influence on how they are read. The reader approaches them with certain religious hopes and expectations. Whatever the original genre of a particular biblical text may have been (e.g., narrative, poem, sermon), the genre of *scripture,* though extrinsic to the author's original purpose, programs the way this text is read, i.e., as the word of God. Although scripture is defined by an act in the past (canonization), it is characterized in the present by the expectations which it arouses, expectations which surpass those which accompany the reading of nonscriptural texts. The Bible functions as a prism

66. Jonathan Culler, *Saussure* (Glasgow: Fontana, 1976), 105.
67. Cf. Marilyn Ferguson, *The Aquarian Conspiracy: Personal and Social Transformation in the 1980s* (Boston: Houghton Mifflin Company, 1980). Chapter 11 is entitled "Spiritual Adventure: Connection to the Source."
68. Nicholson, *Seeing and Reading.*

which refracts the interests, questions, and concerns of the reader into a divine word of consolation and instruction. It is scripture's ability to nourish the soul with present meaning which confirms its standing as a canonical text. If these expectations should ever be dashed over a sufficiently long period of time, the past act of canonization might become virtually a dead letter.

The Bible's effectiveness does not depend upon the reader's ability to infer the intention of the human author. The passage of time has detached the text from the writer, so that its pragmatic effect is no longer subject to the writer's intention. Like other literary texts, the Bible is in the public domain and is measured against something beyond the control of those who produced it.

Biblical interpretation, therefore, cannot be restricted to the restoration of some originally intended message. The change effected in the reader is not necessarily equivalent to the change intended by the writer. The public character of the written text liberates it from any single meaning, even that of the author, and enables the interest of the reader to fill the indeterminacies of the text with present meaning.[69] Readers of the Bible seek to hear "the word of the Lord" addressing them out of the sacred text, as they wrestle with the challenges of daily life. The history of the church, as "the people of the Book," can be said to be the history of biblical interpretation. This history is the story of Bible reading across the centuries, in which it is no easy task to separate the reading from what is read.

THE EXPERIENCE OF READING

WE HAVE COINED the word "empirics" for our study of the experiential dimension of Bible reading. The word is formed by analogy with "hermeneutics," to which it is related but from which it also differs. Hermeneutics is defined as "the study of the principles and rules of interpretation and understanding."[70] The experience of reading may lead to a new interpretation of

---

69. The history of interpretation of the United States Constitution provides an interesting analogy.

70. Frei, *Eclipse of Biblical Narrative,* 9.

the text, but this does not always happen. Moreover, the reading experience may also produce a strong emotional effect, which is not the concern of hermeneutics but is of crucial importance for the reader's transformation.[71] For this transformation involves a new understanding not of the text but of the reader, mediated by the text. This experience conveys not so much an objective, communicable knowledge coming from without (*scientia*) as a transformative knowledge coming from within (*gnosis*).

This is the knowledge to which Paul refers when he describes his purpose in life as being "that I may know Christ and the power of his resurrection" (Phil. 3:10). Such knowledge may be similar to the knowledge received in the mystical state, which consists of insights into depths of truth unplumbed by the discursive intellect. The illuminations and revelations received through reading scripture, though inarticulate, are full of significance and importance to the reader and retain their authority even after the experience is past.[72]

The distinction between "knowing" a person and "knowing about" a person also applies to the reading experience, which elicits not only cognitive but also affective responses. Indeed, the special quality of the knowledge involved makes it very similar to feeling. Engaging the affections provides the energy which leads to transformation. Bible reading leads not only to communicable insights but also to a bliss which cannot be expressed in words. The transformative power of the Bible does not depend upon our ability to give an account of our experience, which may lead simply to wordless adoration. Although the *consequence* of Bible reading may be profoundly ethical, as in the case of Augustine and Antony, the experience itself is private and pre-ethical.[73]

---

71. Cf. Jung, *CW*, vol. 17, 115–16: "The one [way] is a moment of high emotional tension, comparable to the scene in *Parsifal* where the hero, at the very moment of greatest temptation, suddenly realizes the meaning of Amfortas' wound."

72. Cf. James, *Varieties of Religious Experience*, 367.

73. Cf. Roland Barthes, *The Pleasure of the Text*, trans. Richard Miller (New York: Hill and Wang, 1975), 16: "the text . . . manifests the asocial nature of pleasure. . . ." Ibid., 39: "The asocial character of bliss: it is the abrupt loss of sociality. . . ."

Biblical empirics is not limited to those cases mentioned above in which the Bible serves as a catalyst for a sudden conversion or change of life. Biblical empirics includes the *devotional* reading of the text which leads to the *gradual* transformation of the life of the reader. Even those who have undergone sudden conversion experiences continue to read the Bible and to be affected by it.

Biblical empirics also includes those experiences of the text which lead to heightened *political* consciousness. Feminist readings of scripture have cast a new and disturbing light on familiar biblical passages. The point to be noted here is the *interaction* between text and reader. It is not the case that feminist scholars have simply imposed their concerns upon the text. Rather, the patriarchal text itself has, paradoxically, activated these concerns and thereby contributed to its own reinterpretation.

Biblical empirics includes those readings of the Bible through which people living in circumstances of economic and social oppression are emboldened to take action to improve their lot. I recall hearing of a incident in South America where a group who were reading the story of the importunate widow (Luke 18:1–8) resolved to keep pestering a local official until he finally provided the village with an adequate supply of drinking water.[74]

In all these instances it is the emotional energy released through Bible reading which serves to promote change, whether in the reader's spiritual life, in the reader's socioeconomic environment, or in the way in which the text itself is viewed.

The Terror of the Text

READING THE BIBLE is not always a pleasurable experience. The reader will surely experience boredom from time to time,[75] and not infrequently the biblical rhetoric will have an unintended

---

74. See also Ernesto Cardenal, *The Gospel in Solentiname* (Maryknoll, N.Y.: Orbis, 1976).

75. Mark Twain's quip about *The Book of Mormon,* "Chloroform in print," could also be applied to parts of the canonical scripture. Cf. Barthes, *Pleasure of the Text,* 4–5: "This text bores me. It might be said to *prattle*. The prattle of the text is merely that foam of language which forms by the effect of a simple need of writing."

effect upon the modern reader: "What a dreadful tone!"[76] The ranting style of the street preacher, as we encounter it, for example, in the prophet Ezekiel, the "Woes against the Pharisees" (Matt. 23), or the Johannine Jesus, may produce not intimidation and conversion but irritation and exasperation. Biblical empirics includes acknowledging the emotional reactions which the Bible *actually* produces in the reader, not trying to simulate the reactions which the text seems to expect. Nevertheless, if we are able at all to enter into the world of this "horrible" book, the Bible will sooner or later strike terror in the heart. "It is a fearful thing to fall into the hands of the living God" (Heb. 10:31), and it is the living God whose voice we seek to hear in scripture.

The story of King Josiah's discovery of the Book of the Law in the temple is a classic instance of the terror that Bible reading can inspire:

> Great is the wrath of the Lord that is kindled against us, because our fathers have not obeyed the words of this book, to do according to all that is written concerning us (2 Kings 22:13).

John Bunyan refers to "those dreadful Scriptures"[77] which had brought him to the verge of despair. There are countless examples of scripture-based "hell-fire and damnation" sermons which utilize apocalyptic imagery to inspire terror in the congregation and move them to repentance.[78]

In our enlightened age we may regard such reactions to the Bible with condescending amusement, since we are no longer so certain that human disobedience automatically provokes divine retribution, whether here or hereafter. However, even for us the Bible has its terrors. Phyllis Trible has given us a powerful

---

76. Northrop Frye, *The Great Code* (Toronto: Academic Press Canada, 1982), 28: "The essential idiom of the Bible is clearly oratorical, a fact all the more necessary to recognize in an age where there is so well-founded a distrust of the wrong kind of rhetoric. The Bible is often thought to be the wrong kind too: a horrified pre-Revolutionary French lady is said to have remarked, "Quel effroyable ton!" on opening a Bible for the first time."

77. James, *Varieties of Religious Experience,* 192.

78. See, for example, James Joyce, *Portrait of the Artist as a Young Man* (New York: Penguin, 1948), 108–14.

feminist reading of Old Testament stories of the rejection, humiliation, rape, and murder of women—stories which she appropriately calls "texts of terror."[79] The originality of her interpretation discloses an important aspect of biblical empirics: the convergence of the text with a reader who is at a particular level of consciousness produces the experiential impact.

An illustration of this principle may be taken from the interpretation of a New Testament passage. Prior to the rise of feminism, the story of "Joseph's doubt" (Matt. 1:18–25) could be read as a reassuring instance of the God's rescue of the innocent from perilous circumstances. Today, however, it is scarcely possible to read this story without thinking of Mary's tragic vulnerability in a society where a woman's only defense was in a male champion (father, brother, or spouse). The angel's intervention (1:20–21) and the "happy ending" (1:24) do not alleviate this dark scenario.[80]

GOOD NEWS IS NO NEWS

TODAY THERE IS a tendency to limit the Bible's message to whatever affirms the values of our enlightened, democratic society, and to attribute whatever offends against these values to the superstition or patriarchalism of primitive society. This tendency corresponds to the practice of Western theodicy, noted by Jung, of ascribing all good to God and all evil to humanity. But this desire to make God "politically correct" clashes with the experience of God in both testaments and leads to a Pollyanna-like distortion of the God-image. It also ignores God's own declaration in Isa. 45:7: "I form the light, *and create darkness.* I make peace, *and create evil .*" God is beyond good and evil, as God is beyond all human predication. However, the *experience* of God includes both good and evil. Job asks rhetorically, "Shall we receive good at the hand of God, and shall we not receive evil?" (Job 2:10).

Although God is represented in the Bible as the author of the moral law, he does not appear to be bound by this law himself

---

79. Phyllis Trible, *Texts of Terror* (Philadelphia: Fortress, 1984).

80. See Jane Schaberg, *The Illegitimacy of Jesus* (San Francisco: Harper & Row, 1987).

and must be reminded by his own creature, "Shall not the judge of all the earth do right?" (Gen. 18:25). Israel is defeated in battle because of the disobedience of one man (Josh. 7:5), and when the guilty party is discovered, his entire family is stoned along with him (Josh. 7:24–25). Job is cruelly afflicted because God is ignorant of the real motivation behind the hero's blameless conduct (Job 1:8–12). (Job's restoration at the end of the book [Job 42:12–13] does not bring his sons [Job 1:19] back to life.) In the death of Uzzah (2 Sam. 6:6–7) YHWH appears to be not so much immoral as simply amoral; contact with the sacred totem is like touching a high tension wire: the fatal consequences have nothing to do with morality. Despite the exalted moral teaching of the Hebrew Bible, YHWH himself often appears to be ignorant and capricious—a cruel, tribal despot.

The second-century writer Marcion sought to drive a wedge between the two testaments with his sharp distinction between the God of Law and the God of Jesus Christ. It is true that the New Testament projects the shadow side of God onto Satan and his human minions, who are sharply contrasted with the sinless Christ and his faithful followers. However, the New Testament has its own terrors. The crucified Son of God and his vicarious sacrifice for sin evoke the image of the cruel God and inspire dread as well as adoration. Christological exclusivism, which makes incorporation into Christ, through faith and baptism, the sole way to salvation, is a chilling modification of the Old Testament doctrines of election and predestination. The dreadful punishment of Ananias and Sapphira terrifies the Jerusalem church (Acts 5:1–11).

The experience of the Holy includes both horror and fascination, and both of these reactions are elicited by reading the Bible. The cross, which is the unifying symbol of the New Testament books, embraces the opposites: in the cross life and death, crucifixion and resurrection form an indissoluble and paradoxical unity. To hear only "good news" from the pages of holy writ is to truncate its message and to dilute its power.[81] The experience of the biblical God is as varied and conflictual as human experience itself.

---

81. Cf. J. Z. Smith, "Good News Is No News," *Christianity, Judaism, and Other Greco-Roman Cults,* ed. Jacob Neusner (Leiden: Brill, 1975), vol. 1, 21–38.

THE UNKNOWN GOD

THE UNDERLYING ASSUMPTION of the previous paragraph is that the Bible mediates various *images* of God, but that *God* remains unknown and unknowable. In the tradition of Christian mysticism, the basic principle of "apophatic" or "negative" theology is that we can know *that* God is but we cannot know *what* God is, at least not in this life. Christianity introduces a new way of talking about God (cf. Acts 17:23), but this does not and cannot abrogate the agnosticism of biblical religion.

THE EMPIRICS OF INTERPRETATION

BIBLICAL EMPIRICS ENTAILS a shift away from the expectation that biblical interpretation, if pursued in accordance with proper exegetical method, will lead to one "correct" meaning of any given passage. Such univocity of interpretation is called into question by the radically diverse interpretations of modern biblical scholars, all of whom, ostensibly, are using the same method. In the past, both Jewish and Christian interpretive practices recognized *four* distinct senses of scripture. Only with the Enlightenment do we encounter the assumption that the words of scripture can have but one "objective" meaning. This assumption was based on the belief in a human rationality which could be derived from principles quite independent of all social and cultural particularities.[82]

Not all interpretations, of course, are equally interesting or deserve equal attention. However, when the purpose of reading scripture is personal transformation, it is not necessarily the most knowledgeable or ingenious interpretation which is prized. If the value *for the reader* is the primary concern, then the "best" interpretation will be the one which gives the greatest spiritual satisfaction, "for it is not an abundance of knowledge that fills and satisfies the soul but rather an interior understanding and savoring of things."[83]

---

82. Alasdair MacIntyre, *Whose Justice? Which Rationality?* (Notre Dame, Ind.: University of Notre Dame Press, 1988), 6.

83. *The Spiritual Exercises of Saint Ignatius,* trans. Anthony Mottola (Garden City, N.Y.: Doubleday, 1964), 37.

ALLEGORY

ALLEGORY HAS BEEN called an interpretation in which the author supplies the words and the reader supplies the meaning. This accurately describes Paul's interpretation of the Hagar story (Gen. 21) in Gal. 4:21–31, which he explicitly calls an allegory (Gal. 4:24). One reason why this Pauline text is so difficult to interpret is because Paul seems to have projected onto Gen. 21 his own passionate concern with justification by faith, apart from the works of the law. Paul's reading of the Old Testament story does not seem to have arisen out of an open encounter with the text. On the contrary, the apostle finds in the Hagar story precisely what he has put into it.

Such predetermination of meaning has been characteristic of allegory, as it has been practiced in the history of the Christian church. The Hebrew Bible became the scripture of the Christian church partly because it was capable of being interpreted allegorically as referring to Christ. Often allegory has been used to confer meaning on texts which would otherwise have been meaningless or unacceptable for the Christian reader, as Gen. 21 was for Paul. Allegorical interpretation of the Bible has also served to provide "teaching aids" to illustrate the church's doctrine and discipline.

On the other hand, allegory *can* lead to the precise opposite of predetermined meaning: a genuinely open reading may be "allegorical" in the sense that it produces an "other" interpretation, which differs from the way in which the passage in question has previously been understood, even by the same reader. The expectations raised by the scriptural genre will frequently lead the reader to search for a deeper meaning, when the surface meaning fails to provide spiritual satisfaction. Paul dismisses the obvious meaning of Deut. 25:4 with a rhetorical question: "Is it for oxen that God is concerned?" (1 Cor. 9:9). The feminist and liberationist readings to which we have referred are "allegorical" in the sense that they force us to look at the Bible with new eyes.[84]

---

84. See Frances Young, "Allegory and the Ethics of Reading" in *The Open Text,* ed. Francis Watson (London: SMC Press, 1993), 103–20. Also, by the same author, *Virtuoso Theology* (Cleveland, Ohio: Pilgrim Press, 1990).

It is instructive to compare Paul's treatment of the Hagar story with Phyllis Trible's study: "Hagar: the Desolation of Rejection."[85] Paul's manipulation of Gen. 21 seems to be a polemical attempt to turn back on the Judaizers the very text which they had used against him. Although Trible's reading is also polemical and is also motivated by an intense personal concern, it manifests a genuine engagement with the text which enlightens the reader, rather than simply mystifying us. To be sure, the judgment as to whether a particular interpretation is a true reading of the text or simple *eisegesis* ("reading *into* the text") is itself an act of interpretation.

The problem of allegory touches on issues which we shall be discussing later in the book. Here we are concerned with its connection with biblical empirics. When allegory is used to "discover" in the biblical text a pre-existing conviction of the reader, such as Paul's doctrine of justification or the church's rule of faith, then the religious transformation, if it has occurred, is *extrabiblical,* as in the case of Paul's encounter on the Damascus road or of the convert's acceptance of the faith of the church at baptism. When, on the other hand, a new and different interpretation arises out of a genuine encounter with the text, we are dealing with an instance of biblical empirics.

"LEGITIMACY" IN INTERPRETATION

AN EMPIRICAL APPROACH to Bible reading is concerned with what *actually occurs* when a real reader reads the sacred text, rather than with what *ought* to occur, in accordance with "correct" exegetical procedures. An illegitimate child is nonetheless real.

It is considered "illegitimate" because it has come into the world in a manner of which society does not approve. The same can be said of many interpretations of the Bible. They are "illegitimate" because they do not conform with the assumptions, methods, or interests of a particular "interpretive community,"[86] whether this community be ecclesiastical, academic, or political.

---

85. Trible, *Texts of Terror,* 9–35.
86. The phrase comes from Stanley Fish, *Is There a Text in This Class?* (Cambridge: Harvard University Press, 1980).

Such judgments of "illegitimacy" seek to maintain the discipline and control of the regulative group. Feminist critics have seen in the preoccupation with "legitimacy" a reflection of patriarchal culture, in which the husband's concern over whether a child is actually his own is a major source of anxiety. Just as the wayward wife can be ostracized from society, along with her offspring, so the wayward reader and his or her "illegitimate" interpretation can be ostracized by the interpretive community. But this disciplinary action does not undo the deviant interpretation or inhibit its power of attraction. On the contrary, it frequently increases this attraction, as the history of censorship abundantly demonstrates.

Biblical empirics "wants to move from the closed fortresses of believer and skeptic to the community of vision."[87] Those with no claim to the specialized knowledge of the theologian or the biblical scholar and even those without any attachment to institutional religion may yet be drawn to the sacred text by an interest in spiritual adventure or in personal and social transformation. If such a person shares with us his or her reading of a biblical text with which we are familiar, we may be interested, outraged, bored, or perplexed. But we should try to refrain from declaring the reading "illegitimate" or from seeking to undo its effect upon the reader.

The professional knowledge of the biblical scholar may actually inhibit biblical empirics in those who look to the "expert" to tell them "what the Bible really means." Such persons will probably not fully exercise their own capacity for engaging with the text and wrestling from it the meaning they need for their own lives. When a reader projects onto the "expert" a capacity or ability which he or she possesses, we have an example of what Ludwig Feuerbach called "alienation."[88]

Here we touch upon a basic hermeneutical question: Who is competent to interpret the Bible? Other forms of classic literature require special training in order to be properly understood. But if the Bible's function is "to change the blood," that is, to transform

---

87. Frye, *Great Code*, 230.
88. For Feuerbach, religion is the evacuation of people's best qualities and power into the Deity.

the reader by engaging our emotional energy and thus bringing about a shift in equilibrium in the personality, then conceptual understanding and its prerequisites are not of primary concern. We must be prepared to entertain the dangerous notion that anyone who is affected by reading the Bible thereby demonstrates an interpretive competence.

Of course, not all the emotions which Bible reading stirs up in us are the result of an encounter with the Holy, nor are they necessarily commendable, from a moral point of view. One of the important functions of historical criticism has been to counter the religious fanaticism and intolerance which sacred texts sometimes seem to provoke. Before the recent triumph of democracy in South Africa, the Reformed Church in that country used to cite the Bible as justification for apartheid, and Christian fundamentalist groups in the United States claim biblical authority for their thesis that "God hates homosexuals."

Some would say that an interpretation of the Bible which leads to immoral consequences is, by that very fact, "illegitimate." But, as we have seen, the social undesirability of a particular interpretation does not make it go away. It therefore seems preferable to restrict our moral judgment to the *consequences* of interpretation and to maintain an empirical approach to the act of interpretation itself. The principle "By their fruits you shall know them" (Matt. 7:20) does not resolve the hermeneutical issue. The people's cry at Jesus' trial, "His blood be on us and on our children" (Matt. 27:25), has played a fateful role in the history of Jewish–Christian relations. But this troubling fact does not remove the offensive verse from our Bibles or provide us with a benign interpretation of it.

We cannot grasp an emotion in which we have never participated. No one who stands outside the emotion experienced by another person can understand why this emotion has led to extraordinary and unforeseeable consequences. If we ourselves have never experienced the effects of Bible reading which we have been considering in this chapter, then we must limit ourselves to observing those who have had such experiences and to taking their testimony seriously.

*   *   *

THE CONTEXT OF THE READER

ALL INTERPRETATION REQUIRES some sort of context, but the context will vary according to the aims of the interpreter. The historical critic interprets the Bible in the historical context in which the various biblical books were written. The theologian interprets the Bible in the context of his or her confessional system. But what is the context in which the Bible is to be interpreted when the aim in view is the personal transformation of the reader?

J. A Bengel's *Gnomon Novi Testamenti* (1742) begins with the admonition: "Apply yourself to the text, and apply the text to yourself" (my translation). The Bible can only become scripture when it takes on personal significance for the reader. The truth of scripture is always concrete, never merely universal. In what is arguably the most important hermeneutical study written in this century, H.-G. Gadamer affirms the centrality of application for interpretation:

> The interpreter dealing with a traditional text seeks to apply it to himself. [T]he interpreter seeks no more than to understand this universal thing, the text. . . . In order to understand that, he must not seek to disregard himself and his particular hermeneutical situation. He must relate the text to this situation if he wants to understand at all.[89]

For the Bible to be applied to the life of the reader, it must be read in the light of the *reader's* context. The faith of Abraham (Gen. 15:6), "the father of many nations" (Gen. 17:5; Rom. 4:17), took on significance for Paul in the light of the Christian mission to the Gentiles. Luther appropriated Paul's teaching on "justification by faith" *alone* (Rom. 5:1)—the italicized word was added by the Reformer—in the context of his own inability to find peace with God as an Augustinian friar.

The reader's personal context seems to have been crucial in all the instances which we have cited above. Augustine heard Paul's exhortation in the context of the sexual liaison which held him fast. Antony interpreted Jesus' command in relation to the property which he had inherited. Feminist readings of scripture appeared when the equality

---

89. H.-G. Gadamer, *Truth and Method* (New York: Seabury, 1975, 289.

of women was championed and their subjugation to male authority was challenged. The liberationist reading of the Bible in terms of "the preferential option for the poor" arose in response to widespread poverty, both in the Third World and at home.

As these examples show, the reader's context is always personal and unique, but, at the same time, it includes those group ties by which any reader is inevitably affected. By this I do not mean simply membership in a particular church or academic profession. Our interpretation is also affected by whether we are men or women, black or white, rich or poor, gay or straight. The reader may not always be aware of the influence of these group allegiances, but they are nonetheless real. Indeed, an important adjunct of biblical empirics is the ability to reflect upon the interpretations which suggest themselves to us, and to ask ourselves: why have I seen *this* in the text, rather than *that*?

THE VARIETIES OF EXPERIENCE

THE DIFFERENCES IN our experience of reading the Bible are the result not only of our personal situation and group allegiances but also of factors of a specifically psychological nature. William James distinguishes between the "once born" and the "twice born," between "the religion of healthy-mindedness" and "the sick soul."[90]

It would be easy to marshal biblical texts expressing these contrasting religious viewpoints, and they would probably be the same texts invoked by Augustine and Pelagius, respectively, in their bitter dispute over original sin, the theological foundation for the "sick soul" perspective. Augustine's emphasis on the depravity of human nature and the sovereignty of divine grace reappeared with the Protestant Reformers, e.g., in Luther's work *On the Servitude of the Will,* and it persists today wherever Reformed theology retains an influence. "The religion of healthy-mindedness" characterizes modern Western liberalism, across confessional lines.

From a doctrinal perspective, these two positions may be mutually exclusive, but from a psychological point of view, they both have a place. James asks rhetorically:

---

90. James, *Varieties of Religious Experience,* 92–171.

are different functions in the organism of humanity allotted to different types of man, so that some may really be the better for a religion of consolation and reassurance, whilst others are better for one of terror and reproof?[91]

In any case, these contrasting attitudes do exist, and they clearly affect our experience in reading the Bible, particularly insofar as they predispose us to be attracted by certain passages and repelled by others.

PSYCHOLOGICAL DEVELOPMENT

J. A. APPLEYARD[92] HAS made us aware of the psychological changes which affect our experience of reading from childhood to old age. When, as a boy, I stumbled upon the story of Judah and Tamar in the family Bible, the account of a widow dressing up as a prostitute to seduce her father-in-law (Gen. 38:13–19) was a bizarre but unforgettable introduction to "the facts of life." Years later, when I was in graduate studies, the conduct of a woman who was "more righteous" than her father-in-law (Gen. 38:26) and explicitly included as an ancestress of Jesus (Matt. 1:3) would take on quite a different meaning in the context of a Gospel where the theme of "greater righteousness" (Matt. 5:20) is central.

SEPARATE AND CONNECTED KNOWING

IN HER BOOK, *Women's Ways of Knowing,* M. F. Belenky and her associates distinguish between "understanding" and "knowledge," a distinction comparable to the one which we have made between *gnosis* and *scientia*:

> Understanding involves intimacy and equality between self and object, while *knowledge* (*wissen, savoir, saber*) implies separation from the object and mastery over it. Understanding . . . entails acceptance. It precludes evaluation, because evaluation puts the

---

91. Ibid., 327.

92. J. A. Appleyard, *Becoming a Reader* (Cambridge: Cambridge University Press, 1994).

object at a distance, places the self above it, and quantifies a response to the object that should remain qualitative.[93]

Although this distinction evolved out of a situation of interpersonal dialogue, it can be applied to the relationship between the reader and the text. Separate knowledge, which puts the interpreter above the text and in judgment over it, is characteristic of the academic approach to scripture. Connected knowledge is what is involved in biblical empirics.

Belenky's distinction parallels Jung's distinction between *logos* ("reason") and *eros* ("love"). The former is the principle of rational analysis; the latter is the principle of connection. The former seeks to engage the biblical author in a debate; the latter penetrates beneath the offensive rhetoric and archaic worldview to an experience of the Holy, from which sacred scripture is presumed to have originated.

THE NUMINOUS AND THE "INFERIOR" FUNCTION

JUNG'S STUDY ON *Psychological Types*[94] has contributed the words "introvert" and "extravert" to our language. These opposing dispositions are called "attitude types." In addition there are the four "function-types": thinking and feeling; intuition and sensation. In his briefest formulation of the different functions, Jung says:

> *Sensation* (i.e., sense-perception) tells you that something exists; *thinking* tells you what it is; *feeling* tells you whether it is agreeable or not; and *intuition* tells you whence it comes and where it is going.[95]

This psychological typology has been popularized in the Myers–Briggs test.[96] Everyone has a "superior" or "dominant" function, that is, the function which is most highly differentiated and on

93. M. F. Belenky et al., *Women's Ways of Knowing* (New York: Basic Books, 1986), 101.

94. Jung, *CW,* vol. 6.

95. C. G. Jung, *Man and His Symbols* (Garden City, N.Y.: Doubleday, 1964), 61.

96. See Isabel Briggs–Myers with Peter B. Meyers, *Gifts Differing* (Palo Alto, Calif.: Consulting Psychologists Press, 1985).

which a person most relies in his or her conscious activity. These four functions are in paired opposites, so that the function opposed to the "superior" function becomes the "inferior" function, that is, the one least accessible to consciousness. The inferior function is

> undomesticated, unadapted, uncontrolled, and primitive. Because of its contamination with the collective unconscious, it possesses archaic and mystical qualities, and is the complete opposite of the most differentiated function.[97]

If thinking is one's dominant function, then feeling will be the inferior function.

That is actually the case with most academics: the thinking function is what we rely on in our professional work. The interesting point for biblical empirics is that the sense of the numinous comes through the *inferior* function, that is, the function which is most unconscious. This religious significance of the inferior function is a psychological application of the principle contained in the Lord's words to Paul: "My grace is sufficient for you, for *my power is made perfect in weakness*" (2 Cor. 12:9).

An approach to the Bible through the thinking function may be counterproductive from a religious point of view. This is not surprising, since Jung has this to say about the "extraverted thinking type":

> Irrational phenomena such as religious experiences, passions, and suchlike are often repressed to the point of complete unconsciousness.[98]

Only by relaxing the control exercised by the thinking function and by exposing oneself to the unconscious influence of the inferior feeling function can the extraverted thinker expect the Bible to lead to an experience of the Holy. For those of another psychological typology it will work quite differently. For example, a person with a dominant feeling function may sense the numinous in those dimensions of scripture which I have experienced as dry canals, because they primarily involve the thinking function.

---

97. Jung, *CW,* vol. 11, 121.
98. Ibid., vol. 6, 348.

THE ENGLISH BIBLE

FOR BIBLICAL EMPIRICS the function of language is obviously central, and we shall be devoting a chapter to this question. Here we need to address a specific linguistic issue: that of translation. The position of the vernacular Bible in the English church was achieved only after a long history of opposition and conflict. The Wycliffite versions of the Bible, which had been quietly circulating in manuscript among the people since the end of the fourteenth century, were under ecclesiastical censure; the Bible translator William Tyndale was burned at the stake (1536);[99] Miles Coverdale, who produced the first complete English Bible (1535), spent much of his life in exile.

Under the influence of Thomas Cranmer, an official injunction was issued in May 1541 that a copy of the "Great Bible" should be set up in every parish church in England,[100] and in February 1543 the Convocation of Canterbury ordered that on every Sunday and major feast day one chapter of scripture was to be publicly read in English, starting with the New Testament, "and when the New Testament was read over, then to begin with the Old."[101]

Following the English people's first honeymoon with the Bible under Henry VIII, the rapid spread of interest led to further revisions: the Geneva Bible (1560)—the work of English exiles during the reign of Mary, which was the Bible of Shakespeare—and the Bishops' Bible of 1568 and 1572, which was written in reaction to the rigidly Calvinist notes included in the Geneva Bible. The Hampton Court Conference (1604) produced a decision to undertake a new translation of the Bible, and the result was the publication of the world's bestseller, the Authorized Version (1611).

---

99. From Feb. 22–May 17, 1997, the New York Public Library sponsored an exhibit entitled "Let There Be Light: William Tyndale and the Making of the English Bible." At least 70 percent of the Authorized Version is from Tyndale (Neill, *Anglicanism*, 56).

100. Diarmaid MacCulloch, *Thomas Cranmer* (New Haven: Yale University Press, 1996), 283.

101. Quoted in Neill, *Anglicanism*, 58.

Until this century, the so-called "King James Version" *was* the Bible for English-speaking Protestants. It came into being during one of the greatest periods in the history of English literature, and it is, itself, a work of literature, on a par with the plays of Shakespeare. The King James Version is the Bible which has influenced the great figures of English literature, down to the present day, and, like Shakespeare, it has contributed countless expressions to the language we speak, often without our even being aware of the fact. When Northrop Frye wrote *The Great Code,* he chose to quote from the Authorized Version (AV), "except where it is wrong or inadequate."[102]

Frye's decision was partly influenced by the practical consideration that the AV was "the most familiar and accessible version." He did *not* choose it "because of the beauty of its cadences: conventional aesthetic canons of that sort I wanted to get rid of at the start."[103]

From the standpoint of biblical empirics, however, sound is every bit as important as meaning. In the Hindu tradition, spiritual awareness is mediated by the sounds, rhythms, intonations, pitch, and modulations of the ancient Vedic hymns, quite apart from their verbal meaning.[104] In fact, many Brahmans in the nineteenth century recited the hymns by heart, without any understanding of what they meant.[105] Although the disjunction of sound and meaning is not part of the Christian experience, the stately phrasings and haunting cadences of the AV are religiously significant, despite Frye's disclaimer.

Frederick Faber, a convert to Roman Catholicism, lamented the hardship of having to forsake the glories of the AV:

> It lives on the ear like a music that can never be forgotten, which the convert hardly knows how he can forego. Its felicities often seem to be almost things rather than mere words. . . . In the length and breadth of the land there is not a Protestant,

---

102. Frye, *The Great Code,* xiii.
103. Ibid.
104. W. C. Smith, *What Is Scripture?* (Minneapolis: Fortress, 1993), 132.
105. Ibid., 302.

with one spark of religiousness about him, whose spiritual biography is not the Saxon Bible.[106]

According to an Italian saying, *"tradutore tradditore,"* i.e., "the translator is a traitor." If a translation is to be intelligible to its intended audience, it must blend the idiom of the original text with that of its own age. The better the translator, the more subtly he or she will transmute the preconceptions of the ancient text into more familiar ones.[107]

Paradoxically, the translators of the AV achieved this goal by the use of deliberate archaizing. Their diction and idioms were grounded in Tudor English of at least half a century earlier, rather than in Jacobean usage and speech rhythms. This allowed the translators to insure

> the remarkably rapid acceptance of the 1611 translation as not only canonic, but as somehow native to the spirit of the language and as a document uniquely interwoven with the past of English feeling. . . . [C]ountless readers then and since . . . have found a native presence in what is, in obvious truth, a remote, entirely alien world of expression and reference. . . . This . . . would not have occurred had [the translators] laboured to be "modern."[108]

Archaism as a stylistic device was also used in the New Testament. In the Acts of the Apostles Luke employs the old-fashioned linguistic aura of the Septuagint to characterize the period of the church's beginnings as a holy period and to evoke the "good old days" of the apostolic community.[109]

If the response to the Holy comes primarily from the domain of instinct and emotion, as Otto has argued, then the archaizing used by the AV and Luke would have a psychological significance. People do seem to be moved by archaic texts, both

---

106. Quoted in Neill, *Anglicanism,* 135n.

107. MacIntyre, *Whose Justice?,* 18.

108. George Steiner, *After Babel* (New York: Oxford University Press, 1975), 348–49.

109. Schuyler Brown, "Précis of Eckhard Plümacher, *Lukas als hellenistischer Schriftsteller,*" *Society of Biblical Literature 1974 Seminar Papers* (Cambridge, Mass.: SBL, 1974), vol. 2, 105–9.

scriptural and liturgical, for reasons which they themselves may be unable to explain or even to articulate.

Although religious language should be "understood of the people" (The Church of England's Twenty-Fourth Article of Religion), many religious traditions consider it inappropriate, at least in formal situations, to use colloquial language in speaking to or about the Deity. The effect of "holy" language can be achieved by using an earlier, though still intelligible, stage of the vernacular in question.

The English Bible, I believe, is in a transitional period. The modern biblical movement has made us acutely aware of the limitations of the scholarship on which the AV was based, and it has replaced "the Saxon Bible" with an extraordinary proliferation of modern English translations. Most of these versions express the scholarly ideals of historical accuracy, clarity, intelligibility, and, in the last decade, political correctness. These are all important values in our culture, but they do not correspond, necessarily, to the laws of the psyche. The modernizing, rationalizing tendency of most contemporary English Bibles makes them unhelpful from the perspective of biblical empirics. When I hear a modern translation of a familiar passage, such as the Nativity story (Luke 2:1–20) or Paul's hymn in praise of charity [sic] (1 Cor. 13), I may appreciate the fidelity with which the ideas of the original text have been transmitted, but the power of the traditional rendering is no longer there.

Since all translations are "variant readings" of the original, the multiplicity of modern English Bibles can provide an enriching approximation to the original for those who do not know the ancient languages. However, the absence today of any "authorized" English Bible is a disincentive to memorizing the scriptures, a practice which, in all religious traditions, has played a major role in appropriating and experiencing sacred texts.

The goals of biblical scholarship and biblical empirics are different but not contradictory. It may therefore be advisable, for the present, to use two different translations, one for study purposes (where conceptual clarity is the ideal) and the other for devotion. However, I hope that one day we may have a translation which meets the criteria for both uses of the Bible. As Nathan Mitchell observes in his review of the ICEL Psalter,

> to be faithful and true, a translation must reach beyond words and referents to images (acoustic *and* visual); to memory and mystery; to the thoughtful creation of spaces.[110]

The biblical scholar views a translation *diachronically*, that is, from the perspective of where it came from. A translation is therefore considered secondary and derivative and is evaluated according to its "fidelity to the original." But a translation may also be viewed *synchronistically*, that is, as an autonomous work, to be judged only by itself and its effect on the reader. My high school Greek teacher once startled me by saying that he thought that the Loeb Library translation of Aristophanes was "better than the original." This, of course, is nonsense, if a translation is simply a medium through which another text is imperfectly understood. But it makes perfect sense if a translation is considered as a creation in its own right and then compared with the original text, as one work of art with another.

In such a comparison, "mistranslations" are no grounds for a negative judgment. One of the most famous lines of the AV contains such a mistranslation: "Yea, though I walk through the valley of the shadow of death, I will fear no evil" (Ps. 23:4). Viewed as an autonomous work of art, "The Lord is my Shepherd" is

> a profound and spiritually transcendent poem, universally known as is perhaps no other lyric in our tongue, and now entered permanently in the canon of English poetry.[111]

The Greek Septuagint, the version of the Old Testament which the New Testament authors knew and cited, is full of such "mistranslations," the most famous being the use of the Greek word for "virgin" (*parthenos*) in place of the Hebrew word for

---

110. *Worship,* 69 (1995), 449.
111. Willis Barnstone, *The Poetics of Translation* (New Haven: Yale University Press, 1993), 105.

"young woman" *(almah)* in Isa. 7:14 (cf. Matt. 1:23). The centrality of the Septuagint for Christianity led to the view that it was inspired, and this claim makes the similar claim for the AV seem less absurd. Indeed, if the charism of inspiration includes the power of inspiring the reader, then, perhaps, it should not be denied to scriptures in languages which are in current use.

Revelation, as the living word of God, is appropriately communicated in living language. When the languages in which the original texts of scripture were written fell into disuse, these texts were followed by Aramaic targums, the Greek Septuagint, and subsequent vernacular versions. For the work of scholarship the original texts are of primary importance, but it is the vernacular versions, including the English Bible, which have had, and continue to have, an immediate impact upon the life of the church.

CONCLUSION

IN THIS CHAPTER we have been dealing with a phenomenon with which people are generally aware but which has, to my knowledge, not become a focus of much sustained reflection. Perhaps this is because biblical empirics is judged to be too subjective to be amenable to any sort of scholarly treatment.

To such a judgment, two things must be said. First of all, it must be emphasized that "subjective" does not mean "arbitrary." *All* interpretation is subjective, since its point of departure is the interpreter. Secondly, the response to the Bible with which we have been dealing in this chapter, though unpredictable, is not arbitrary. As we shall see, it is governed by the laws both of language and of the psyche.

Of course, biblical empirics is only one part of the picture. The Bible attests to the process of rationalization and moralization which characterizes all religion. In analyzing these aspects of the Bible, the reasoning faculty, which is the dominant one in the scholarly community, has its work cut out for it. However, the reconstruction of origins, the analysis of doctrine, and the evaluation of ethical teaching do not, of themselves, produce the transformative effects which have been our concern. For that to happen, the affective element must be present, creating not only new interpretations but also renewed lives.

2. Literary Criticism

Every scribe who has been trained for the kingdom of heaven is like a householder who brings out of his treasure what is new and what is old.
—Matt. 13:52

NEW CRITICISM

THE RELEVANCE OF literary criticism for biblical empirics is the result of developments within literary criticism itself. Literary criticism used to operate from the same assumption which governs biblical studies today, i.e., that a work of literature can only be properly understood when we have studied the environment in which it was written. But in Anglo-American literary criticism, from the late 1930s through the 1950s, a movement arose which challenged this assumption. This movement was called New Criticism. The New Critics insisted on the autonomy of the literary work. The meaning of a work comes from the work itself, not from its historical context or the intention of its author.

This position calls to mind Luther's formulation, *scriptura sui interpres* ("scripture interprets itself"), as well as Cranmer's view that the scriptural word of God comes with the greatest power when unaccompanied by any human gloss, comment, or exposition. New Criticism's view of the text also corresponds to Hugh of St. Victor's metaphor of the "vineyard": the text is to be tilled for the reader's profit and pleasure;[112] it has not yet become a storehouse of promptly usable, well-coined knowledge.[113] For New Criticism, as for Hugh, form and content are inseparable. The text is not a vehicle for a content which could be separated from it.

---

112. Illich, *Vineyard of the Text,* 57.
113. Ibid., 96.

For the Reformers the autonomy of scripture meant the exclusion of ecclesiastical formulations as a norm for interpretation. Luther believed that even councils could err. For the New Critics, it is the historical background of a work which is excluded as a norm for interpretation. Applied to the Bible, this means that although a knowledge of the social world from which the Bible came may greatly expand our knowledge of what the Bible *meant*, this does not determine what the Bible *means* for the contemporary reader.[114] Appreciation of the vernacular Bible does not require familiarity with the cultural milieus in which the ancient originals were written. No appeal need be made in interpretation to anything outside the text: the Bible confronts the reader with the same immediacy as Jesus' preaching, and with the same exhortation: "He who has ears to hear, let him hear!" (Mark 4:9).

PRIVATE INTERPRETATION

NEW CRITICISM'S DOCTRINE of the text's autonomy "became such an absolute that the notion that a reader's responses to a poem or story might be pertinent to understanding it was labeled a 'fallacy' in an influential essay by Wimsatt and Beardsley (1954)."[115] For us the exclusion of extrinsicism from interpretation moves in quite the opposite direction: it means that the responsibility for interpretation falls squarely on the reader. In the words of the Canadian writer Timothy Findley,

> Books, like dreams, are essentially private realms. Nothing should be allowed to detract from each person's right to read a book privately and to interpret it freely in the light of what each person has experienced and knows of life.[116]

---

114. This distinction, which goes back to Krister Stendahl, has been challenged by "the new historicism" and is called "dated and fragile" by John Donahue ("The Literary Turn and New Testament Theology," *Journal of Religion* 76/2 [April 1996], 271). However, for the purposes of this book, whose perspective is rather different, the distinction is still a useful one.

115. Appleyard, *Becoming a Reader,* 6.

116. Afterword to Margaret Lawrence, *The Diviners* (Toronto: McLelland and Stewart, 1988), 491.

Findley's comparison of books and dreams makes applicable to biblical empirics what Jung affirmed about a dream of one of his analysands:

> In such a case it does not matter at all what *our* impression is or what *we* think about it. It only matters how the patient feels about it. It is *his* experience, and if it has a deeply transforming influence upon his condition there is no point in arguing against it.[117]

Critics of the text, whether they represent the church, the literary establishment, or biblical scholarship, can have a useful function, but, in the last analysis, they speak only for themselves, and they cannot invalidate the individual reader's interpretation.

In fact, it is only the individual who *can* interpret the text. The quest for meaning is not a collective enterprise. Groups may come to an agreement as to how texts are to be read, and individuals are free to accept such group decisions. But a group, as such, does not interpret. Even when scripture is read aloud to a congregation, it is received and understood by the individuals who make up that congregation, and there may be as many interpretations within any given congregation as there are members present.

SECTARIAN INTERPRETATION

THERE IS ONE instance of extrinsicism in interpretation with which the New Critics were *not* concerned, but which is definitely a problem for biblical empirics. In the Acts of the Apostles we have the story of the Ethiopian eunuch who was reading the Book of Isaiah as he rode along in his chariot on pilgrimage to Jerusalem. Philip the Evangelist, moved by the spirit, runs up to the chariot and inquires, "Do you understand what you are reading?" The eunuch replies, "How can I, unless someone guides me?" (Acts 8:30–31). Philip then proceeds to tell him "the good news of Jesus" (Acts 8:35).

---

117. Jung, *CW,* vol. 11, 65.

This story illustrates the reader's abdication of responsibility as an interpreter and his befuddled deferral to a supposedly better-informed expert. However, the scene also expresses, in narrative form, the conviction common to all the writers of the New Testament that the Jewish scriptures have to do with Jesus Christ. In the Fourth Gospel the Johannine Jesus says to his Jewish opponents:"You search the scriptures, because you think that in them you have eternal life, and it is they that bear witness to me" (John 5:39).

Now there is nothing outlandish in such a use of scripture in the context of first-century Jewish sectarianism, and we need to remember that the Christian church started out as a Jewish sect (cf. Acts 24:5.14; 28:22). Within the Qumran community the Bible was interpreted in very much the same way. The prophet Habbakuk is understood to be writing about the persecution of the sect and its leader, the Teacher of Righteousness, by "the House of Absolom" (probably the Pharisees are meant):

> Interpreted, this (Hab. 1:13b) concerns the House of Absolom
> and the members of its council who were silent at the time of
> the chastisement of the Teacher of Righteousness and gave him
> no help against the Liar who flouted the Law in the midst of
> their whole [congregation].[118]

However, for biblical empirics in the twentieth century, such sectarian interpretation is a problem, not so much because a work is being interpreted apart from its historical context, but rather because a Christian evangelist is presuming to tell a Jew what his or her scriptures *really* mean. After the Holocaust this seems completely inappropriate. The assumption that Jewish scripture can only be understood in the light of the Christian gospel (cf. 2 Cor. 3:12–18) is not only offensive in an ecumenical situation; it also undermines the autonomy of the Old Testament as the word of God.

---

118. Geza Vermes, *The Dead Sea Scrolls in English* (Baltimore: Penguin Books, 1965), 238.

At the same time, I have to acknowledge that for Christians who have come to know the Old Testament[119] through the New,[120] a Christian understanding of Old Testament texts is natural and per- haps even inevitable. In a performance of Handel's *Messiah*, where texts from both testaments are stitched together to celebrate the Christian story, a christological understanding of the Old Testament passages seems neither contrived nor offensive.

I must return to the point which I made in the discussion of allegory. If a christological interpretation of the Old Testament arises out of the reading experience itself, then we have an instance of biblical empirics. But if the biblical text is manipulat- ed for the sake of "proving" the Christian dogma, then something quite different is involved. My concern is not with "legitimacy" but with the process by which an interpretation has arisen: whether meaning has been *produced* or merely *assigned.*[121]

I certainly would not wish to exclude the influence of Christian faith in reading the Old Testament, provided the interpretation which results is not put forward as the one and only meaning of the text.

By the same token, Roman Catholics reading the "Thou art Peter" text in Matt. 16:18–19 will naturally hear a reference to the Petrine office which occupies so central a place in their faith. The same may be said of the application of texts such as Prov 8:22–36 or Revelation 12:1–6 to the Virgin Mary. I take such interpretations to be instances

---

119. Some Christian scholars avoid the term "Old Testament," since they think that "old" implies "superseded." However, Jewish scholars point out that "Old Testament" is *implied* by "New Testament," whether the former term is used or not. Moreover, the Old Testament differs from the Hebrew scriptures in the order of the individual books, and this entails a difference in interpretation. The Old Testament concludes with the sending of Elijah the prophet (Mal. 4:5–6; cf. Luke 1:17). The Hebrew Bible concludes with Cyrus' exhortation to "go up" to rebuild the temple in Jerusalem (2 Chron. 36:23).

120. Such a hermeneutic is not peculiar to Christianity. Prof. W. C. Smith has remarked: "The Talmud cannot be considered a commen- tary on the Bible, but the Bible might be considered a commentary on the Talmud."

121. Culler, *Saussure*, 113.

of biblical empirics, not of *eisegesis*. However, it is not to be expected that those of another faith persuasion will find them attractive. As F. W. Burnett has written, "readers operate already within a discursive system of reading conventions which allows certain readings (meanings) to be actualized and others to be excluded."[122]

We should not assume too easily that we are able to distinguish between the "literal sense" or the "intention of the author" and reading conventions which we may have accepted quite unconsciously. In early Jewish exegesis what was designated as the *peschat*, i.e., the "plain" sense, was often not the natural meaning of the text but the one familiar from traditional teaching, which the community recognized as authoritative.[123]

WHAT IS A TEXT?

ALTHOUGH THE PRINCIPLE of "the autonomy of the text" effectively excludes extrinsicism in interpretation, it leaves unanswered the question: What is a text? Strictly speaking, Luther's view that "scripture interprets itself" is nonsense: texts do not interpret; only human beings interpret.

The idea that texts are autonomous may have arisen from the simple fact that books are physical objects: we can put them on the shelf and forget about them, until the time comes when we need to consult one of them. But books as physical objects are simply ink on paper; books as texts are a different matter. A text has to do with meaning, and meaning is not a physical property.

When meaning is at issue, we cannot even think of a text apart from those who produced it and those who interpret it. As a bearer of meaning, a text implies both the complex processes which brought it into existence and the mysterious reactions which it elicits. A text, as a literary artifact, involves both production and

---

122. F. W. Burnett, "Characterization and Christology in Matthew," *Society of Biblical Studies 1989 Seminar Papers* (Atlanta, Ga.: Scholars Press, 1989), 588.

123. Raphael Loewe, "The 'Plain' Meaning of Scripture in Early Jewish Exegesis," *Papers of the Institute of Jewish Studies London I* (Jerusalem, 1964), 140–85.

consumption. Without an author or authors the text would not exist; without readers the text could not be interpreted.

AUTHOR, TEXT, AND INTERPRETATION

BUT WHAT BEARING does the author have on the text's interpretation? Some texts simply substitute for oral communication. If I receive a memo from my college dean saying, "Please see me in my office tomorrow at nine o'clock," the authorial intention is so obvious that I have virtually no room for interpretation, although I may speculate about why the message was sent. Moreover, the memo itself has no significance apart from the message it contains. Once I have gotten the message, I can throw the memo in the trash.

Revelation is often understood in terms of oral speech ("The word of the Lord came unto me, saying. . . ."). However, this revelation is preserved in literary texts, which are as different from office memos as they are from the spoken word. Although the author must have had some intention in writing a work (e.g., political or religious propaganda, moral improvement of the readers, entertainment), this intention, even if it could be deduced from reading the work, *need* not influence the reader in interpreting the work, and it usually *does* not do so.

The meaning of words is the meaning they *can* have in the interpersonal linguistic system from which they emerge.[124] The capacity of a text to generate multiple, even contradictory, meanings lies not only in the social character of language but also in the nature of the text itself:

> Every text is an intertext; other texts are present in it, at variable levels, in more or less recognizable forms: the texts of the previous culture and those of the surrounding culture. Every text is a new fabric woven out of bygone quotations.[125]

---

124. Culler, *Saussure,* 113.
125. Roland Barthes, "Texte, [Théorie du]," *Encyclopaedia Universalis* (Paris, 1973), vol. 15, 1015 (trans. Lyle Eslinger).

This is true even of contemporary texts, whose authors are still alive and can be consulted. Their testimony to the text's meaning, though interesting, is not authoritative; it imposes no obligation on the reader. In the case of ancient texts, such as the Bible, the restriction of interpretation to the recovery of the author's intention is even less appropriate.

A foundational text like the Bible elicits countless new meanings, as it is read in ever-changing circumstances which its human authors could never have imagined. (The American Constitution functions in similar fashion.) The social function of such a text makes its meaning necessarily open-ended, as the ongoing history of interpretation makes abundantly clear. A Puritan divine once declared, "God hath yet more truth to come forth from his holy word." The doctrine of divine inspiration, which expands the possible meanings of scripture beyond anything which the human authors could ever have conceived, provides theological justification for such open-endedness.

This poses a problem for historical and doctrinal interpretation, both of which, in different ways, seek closure and determinacy of meaning. When exegetes appeal to "the original meaning," which they deduce through their own interpretive efforts, they may be projecting their own interest in the text upon long deceased and often anonymous authors, who are incapable of responding. "No one can ever grasp exactly what another person might have had in mind, especially if the various distances which separate them are great. . . ."[126] It seems preferable to withdraw the projections and to acknowledge the reader's own contribution to the interpretive process.

THE ROLE OF THE READER

UNDOUBTEDLY THE MOST important development in literary criticism, from the perspective of biblical empirics, is the recognition that the meaning of a text arises out of the reading experience. It is not a "given," located in the mind of the author or in the structure of the text itself. Wolfgang Iser has written:

---

126. Culler, *Saussure,* 110.

> The convergence of text and reader brings the literary work into existence, and this convergence can never be precisely pinpointed, but must always remain virtual, as it is not to be identified either with the reality of the text or with the individual disposition of the reader.[127]

The role of the reader was already implied in the scholastic adage that "whatever is received is received according to the manner of the one receiving it." The English reformer John Wyclif believed that

> the first condition for the student of Scripture, exceeding any capacity he may have for disputation or logical speculation, is a basic godly morality which will prompt him to seek a just interpretation of the text.[128]

The "conflict of interpretations" between Jews and Christians and between divergent Christian groups concerning the same biblical text raises the question of the reader's role in generating meaning, since the scriptural word of God evidently does not have the univocity which is characteristic of doctrinal formulations.

In such sectarian disputes, the "deviant" interpretation is usually represented as a *mis*interpretation, caused by a hardening of the minds of the readers (2 Cor. 3:14), who "twist" the scriptures (2 Pet. 3:16) for their own purposes. Such moral judgments are not usually made by modern scriptural scholars, who still tend, nonetheless, to regard interpretations which differ from their own as *mis*interpretations.

Quoting Iser once again,

> The fact that completely different readers can be differently affected by the "reality" of a particular text is ample evidence of the degree to which literary texts transform reading into a creative process that is far above mere perception of what is written.[129]

---

127. Wolfgang Iser, "The Reading Process," *New Literary History 3* (1972), 279.

128. D. L. Jeffrey, "John Wyclif and the Hermeneutics of Reader Response," *Interpretation 39* (1985), 274.

129. Iser, "Reading Process," 283.

"Reader response criticism" approaches the issue of diversity in interpretation in two different ways. The first approach is a continuation of the Western aesthetic attitude which studies texts in terms of their rhetoric, i.e., their ability to produce effects in their readers.[130] Since most of scripture can be regarded as religious propaganda, which seeks to instill certain beliefs or modes of conduct in the reader, this rhetorical approach seems obvious enough. The emphasis is then on "the reader in the text," that is, the reader implied by those "objective" textual features which guide the actual reader to a "proper" understanding. This approach perpetuates a historical perspective under different terminology: "the implied reader" is really a reflection of "the intention of the author" projected back upon the text.

But what if actual readers do not follow these textual indications, whether through deliberate resistance to such guidance or because they are affected by other dimensions of the text which they find more interesting or personally relevant?[131] In our post-Christian era there are many persons unassociated with either church or synagogue who read the Bible not out of deference to institutional religious authority but out of an interest in "spiritual adventure" and personal and moral transformation, or simply because the Bible is a classic text whose continuing influence, for weal or woe, cannot be ignored.

Rather than dismiss such independent readings of the Bible as misreadings,[132] reader response criticism may adopt another, empirical approach, which encourages actual readers to record their "stories of reading" and which analyzes the reading process phenomenologically. In such an approach, which is obviously the more promising one for biblical empirics, psychological, social, and developmental factors are considered not as intrusive distortions of the reading process but rather as essential components of it.

---

130. Appleyard, *Becoming a Reader*, 4–5.

131. Ibid., 1: "I discovered that most of the college students I was teaching used literature for purposes that my classroom canons of interpretation (not to mention the even stricter theories of contemporary critics) had obliged me to disavow."

132. Cf. Jonathan Culler, *On Deconstruction* (Ithaca: Cornell University Press, 1982), 176: "all readings are misreadings."

The wide range of responses to the Bible is easier to account for if we emphasize the creative imagination which comes to expression in the sacred text, rather than the rhetorical intent which lies behind its composition. Then the creativity of the interpreter may be seen to correspond to the creativity of the author.

READING AS DIALOGUE BETWEEN TEXT AND READER

THE UNPREDICTABILITY OF interpretation can best be appreciated if we imagine the reading process as a dialogue, such as takes place between two persons. The experience of reading as dialogical goes all the way back to our earliest childhood, when we were *read to*.

> Typically the reading is accompanied by a running exchange of questions and answers, comments about the story, and references to other experiences of the child and the reader and to people they know[133]

The young child experiences reading as "a lively interaction between text and reader."[134]

The outcome of a dialogue is necessarily unpredictable, since I cannot know in advance what the response of my dialogue partner will be to what I say, or how I will react to this response. But does it make any sense to speak of having a "dialogue" with a "fixed" text? Actually, the fixity of the text is only apparent. To be sure, the position of the markings on the page does not change as a result of my reading, but the text, as a conveyor of meaning, only comes into existence when it is read. Even those "objective" features of the text such as semantic meaning, connotation, implication, and syntax are not "there" independently of a reader. They have to be recognized; they come into being only through interpretation.

If the meaning of a work is the reader's experience of it, where does the text's contribution to the generation of meaning leave off and the reader's contribution begin? The impossibility of answering this question brings out the dialogical character of the reading experience. After a dialogue with another person, I am often

---

133. Appleyard, *Becoming a Reader,* 21.
134. Ibid., 22.

unable to say *who* contributed *what* to the resulting change in attitude of the dialogue partners. But if interpretation is the expression of what happens to the reader while reading, does this mean that the text disappears behind the creative role of the reader? Although critics sometimes speak as though this were the case, at other times they speak of the text provoking certain responses and actively controlling the reader.

This switch can take place even within a single critical article. Writing for the *Encylopaedia Universalis*, Roland Barthes declares, "[I]t is the text which works untiringly, not the artist or the consumer,"[135] but on the very next page he appears to affirm just the opposite: "the theory of the text removes all limits to the freedom of reading (authorizing the reading of a past work from an entirely modern standpoint)."[136] If the reader can be said to produce meanings, the text can be said to disrupt the reader's most basic conceptions. The very fact that a reader can be surprised or amused by what he or she reads indicates that there are limits to our autonomous creativity. The dialogue between text and reader is an interchange which we have all experienced. We can reflect on it and analyze it to a certain extent, but it remains mysterious.

LANGUAGE AND LITERATURE

THE CLOSE CONNECTION between language and literature is evident from the fact that "philology" has been understood, at various times, to refer to both. It is therefore natural that changes in the approach to language have affected the approach to literature, with important consequences for biblical empirics.

The founder of modern linguistics, Ferdinand de Saussure, understood language to be "a complex equilibrium of reciprocally defined and conditioned terms."[137] This placed the emphasis in language study on the *synchronic* perspective, i.e., the study of the linguistic system in a particular state, without reference to time. The *diachronic* or historical study of language was given a quite secondary and derivative status; language is

---

135. Barthes, "Texte," 1015 (trans. Jonathan Culler).
136. Ibid., 1016.
137. Quoted in Culler, *Saussure,* 47.

no longer understood in terms of the temporal development through which it has reached a particular state or condition, e.g., twentieth-century English.

Applied to literature, a synchronic emphasis means that only the final text is of interest for literary study. The quest for sources diverts attention from the literary work itself, where source and influence are subsumed in the final synthesis. How a text came into existence has no bearing on its interpretation. Such a view of the text is clearly implied by biblical empirics, whose object is the vernacular Bible, and not the hypothetical stages through which the Bible attained its present form.

STRUCTURE, LANGUAGE, AND THE UNCONSCIOUS

THE STRUCTURALIST APPROACH of modern linguistics has led to a school of literary criticism, particularly in France, which some scholars have found applicable to biblical interpretation. However, the relevance for biblical empirics of structuralist approaches to literature is limited. Indeed, concentration on literary codes and systems of signification may lead to overlooking those unconscious processes which are at work both in writing and in reading literature. Structuralism's chief significance is to have secured for the French critics who use it "some of the benefits of Anglo-American 'New Criticism' without leading to the error of making the individual text an autonomous object that should be approached with a *tabula rasa*."[138]

What *is* of particular significance for biblical empirics is the *unconscious* nature of linguistic structure. The notion of the unconscious, which is so central for depth psychology, whether Freudian or Jungian, is demonstrated most clearly and irrefutably in language: I know a language, in the sense of being able to produce and understand new utterances, without knowing *consciously* the linguistic system by which these utterances are governed.[139] Language has been called "rule-governed creativity" (Noam

---

138. Jonathan Culler, *Structuralist Poetics* (Ithaca: Cornell University Press, 1975), 255.

139. Culler, *Saussure,* 76.

Chomsky),[140] but the linguistic rules which any native speaker will *use* correctly may require the help of a professional linguist to be fully elucidated. I *know* whether a particular English formulation is correct or incorrect, even if I cannot say *why*.

The structural unconscious of language arises out of the psyche, which has its own unconscious structure. As we shall see in a later chapter, the interaction of these two unconscious systems affects the way in which the Bible is read and understood. The structure of the text depends upon both the structure of language and the structure of the psyche.

RELATIVITY, DECONSTRUCTION, AND THE MARGIN OF THE TEXT

SAUSSURE'S ANALYSIS OF language reflects a pervasive shift in modern thought: it is relationships which define objects, not the other way around. In the words of Alfred North Whitehead, "every entity is to be understood in terms of the way it is interwoven with the rest of the universe."[141]

In the case of language, this means that "brown" is not some absolute essence; its meaning is given only in relation to the other terms with which it is contrasted: "brown" is what is not blue or red or green or black, and so forth.

Saussure's view that the reality of the linguistic sign is purely relational leads to a relational understanding of reading. Just as the meaning of the linguistic signifier is not to be found in the signifier itself but in the "space" between it and the contrasting signifiers which define it, so the meaning of a text is to be found not in the text itself but in the interaction between text and reader.

Moreover, if the most precise characteristic of every sign is that it differs from other signs, then every sign in some sense bears the traces of all the other signs; they are co-present with it as the entities which define it.[142] No element in language can function as a sign without relating to another element which is not itself present.

---

140. Quoted in Culler, *Saussure,* 83.
141. Ibid., 115.
142. Ibid., 111.

This means that every linguistic element is constituted by the trace of something absent. Nothing in language is ever simply there.

The relational nature of meaning has an important consequence for the interpretation of literature: what appears to be in the forefront of a text depends upon what has been relegated to the margin. "Center" and "margin" define each other reciprocally, as do contrasting colors, but the nature of the relationship between the center and the margin of a text is hierarchical. The interpreter articulates this hierarchy by determining what is "central" in the text and what is "marginal."[143]

"A deconstruction always has for its target to reveal the existence of hidden articulations and fragmentations within assumedly monadic totalities."[144] Deconstruction can reverse the hierarchy between "center" and "margin," so that the central becomes marginal and the marginal central.[145] According to Jacques Derrida,

> the West has categorized phenomena differentially or oppositionally, but it has not been content simply to differentiate one phenomenon from another and then to oppose one to the other. The West has also *privileged* one phenomenon *over* another.[146]

IMAGE AND CONCEPT

THE HIERARCHICAL REVERSAL which is most important for biblical empirics is the relation between image and concept. Both in

---

143. Culler, *Deconstruction*, 140.

144. Paul de Man, *Allegories of Reading* (New Haven: Yale University Press, 1979), 249. We have already referred to the deconstructive effect of historical criticism when applied to biblical doctrine.

145. In the psyche, which Jung believed to be a self-regulating system, there is a corresponding reversal: "The archdemon of egoism leads us along the royal road to that ingathering which religious experience demands. What we observe here is a fundamental law of life—*enantiodromia* or conversion into the opposite; and it is this that makes possible the reunion of the warring halves of the personality and thereby brings the civil war to an end." (Jung, *CW,* vol. 11, 342)

146. M. V. Adams, Deconstructive Philosophy and Imaginal Psychology" in R. P. Sugg, *Jungian Literary Criticism* (Evanston, Ill.: Northwestern University Press, 1992), 233.

biblical studies and in psychology there is a pervasive tendency to reduce the image to a concept, to what it "means" in hermeneutic terms.[147] We have already noted that the search for the "meaning" of the Gospel parables seems to imply that the imagery of the parables is superfluous. "The discovery of the kerygma or proclamation behind the narrative," which was "at the basis of [Rudolf] Bultmann's understanding of the task and structure of New Testament theology,"[148] is a classic case of the reductionistic conceptualization of the imagination. For Bultmann, New Testament theology's primary task is *"setting forth the theological thoughts of the New Testament writings"* and assuring that these *"be conceived and explicated as thoughts of faith."* [149]

In psychology too, "Images are turned into predefined concepts such as passivity, power, sexuality, anxiety, femininity. . . ."[150] James Hillman has taken the lead in reversing this hierarchy, and has protested even against Jung's hermeneutical tendency to privilege the conceptual over the imaginal:"We sin against the imagination whenever we ask an image for its meaning, requiring that images be translated into concepts."[151]

The implication for biblical empirics is obvious: it may be necessary to resist the hermeneutical drive for conceptual meaning and to stay with the image, which is where the transformative energy resides.

MASCULINE AND FEMININE

IN ANDROCENTRIC BIBLICAL texts the feminine will be found, if at all, at the "margin" of the text. But the importance of the feminine for religious discourse may lie in the very things which led to its being relegated to the margin. Since the nature of language is differential (meaning resides in differences), the relationship between masculine and feminine in biblical interpretation can be

---

147. Ibid., 240.

148. Donahue, "The Literary Turn," 251.

149. Ibid., 252.

150. James Hillman, *Re-Visioning Psychology* (New York: Harper & Row, 1977), 8.

151. Ibid., 39.

reversed, so that the feminine becomes central and the masculine marginal. This reversal subverts the distinction between central and marginal, between essential and nonessential, for what *is* a center, if the marginal can become central?[152]

In her study of Matthew's Gospel,[153] Elaine Guillemin has recovered a network of feminine imagery which, because it is "marginal," is easily overlooked. It begins with "the mother and foremothers of the Christ" (Matt. 1:3 [Tamar], 5 [Rahab, Ruth], 6 [the wife of Uriah], 16 [Mary]); it continues with Rachel as *mater dolorosa* ("sorrowful mother") [2:18; cf. Jer. 31:15], Sophia (11:19; 12:42; 13:54), and Jerusalem as *mater crudelis* ("cruel mother") [23:37a]; it culminates in the androgynous image of Jesus as a "mother hen" (23:37b).

This analysis is certainly not "scripture interpreting itself." On the contrary, this network of imagery would probably suggest itself only to someone so deeply alienated by the androcentric emphasis of the text, as conventionally interpreted, that she had to find a way to resist the "obvious" meaning. Resistant reading is an important strategy in feminist literary criticism. It is "a self-defensive measure designed to clear imaginative space beyond the influential web of the traditional script."[154]

Guillemin's interpretation comes from a woman's determination to find in Matthew a revelatory meaning *for women.* But the significance of her analysis is not for women only, for when the androcentrism of the Gospel is reversed, the integrity of the archetype is restored. As a union of opposites, the archetypal image, of Revealer or of Savior, necessarily includes both masculine and feminine.

THEME AND NARRATIVE

MODERN LINGUISTICS HAS distinguished between two different kinds of relationships in language. Those relationships in which linguistic elements can be combined are called *syntagmatic*,

---

152. Culler, *Deconstruction,* 140.

153 Elaine Guillemin, "Female Imagery in Matthew's Gospel" (unpublished dissertation).

154. Willi Braun, "Resisting John," *Studies in Religion* 19 (1990), 64.

relationships of contrast, in which one element can replace another, are called *paradigmatic*. Applied to literature, this distinction yields two axes of interpretation: the horizontal axis of narrative and the vertical axis of theme. The two are so intimately related that "we could say that plot is but the temporal projection of thematic structures."[155] If Guillemin's interpretation of Matthew's Gospel seems arbitrary, that may be because it is a paradigmatic or thematic reading, which foregrounds the vertical axis.

The two axes (narrative and thematic) have a relevance for biblical empirics, since the effects of reading are of two kinds: cognitive and affective. Cognitive effects of reading the Bible seem related to the narrative reading axis. Jesus' preferred form of narrative, the parable, only "works" when the reader (or hearer) sees him- or herself in the story: "You are the man!" (2 Sam. 12:7). Affective responses, referred to in the spiritual tradition as "consolation" or "desolation," would seem to be the effect of powerful, sometimes disconcerting images which have been woven into the text and which speak directly to the unconscious.[156] A sudden change of mood, for which the reader can assign no obvious cause,[157] suggests a psychological influence emanating from the text, a hidden quality that can no more be defined or explained than the quality of a person's speaking voice.

JESUS AND NICODEMUS

THE HORIZONTAL AND vertical axes can be illustrated by Jesus' dialogue with Nicodemus (John 3).[158] This piece of anti-Jewish propaganda is a veritable tissue of archetypal polarities: above/below,

---

155. Culler, *Structuralist Poetics*, 224.

156. Appleyard, *Becoming a Reader*, 37,

157. Cf. the first line of *The Merchant of Venice*, "In truth, I know not why I am so sad," or the line from Heinrich Heine's poem, "Die Lorelei," which means the same thing:

> Ich weiss nicht, was soll es bedeuten
> Dass ich so traurig bin.

158. Schuyler Brown, "John and the Resistant Reader," *Journal of Literary Studies*, vol. 5, no. 3/4 (December 1989), 252–61.

birth/rebirth, water/spirit, spirit/flesh, spirit/wind, earthly/heavenly, ascent/descent, serpent/eternal life, God/world, belief/judgment, light/darkness, evil/truth, bride/bridegroom, increase/decrease, words/spirit, Father/Son, life/wrath. These polarities mediate a powerful experience to the reader, despite the offensive rhetoric of the horizontal axis. Indeed, it is precisely the power of the text which makes the rhetoric so insidious.

The rhetoric seeks to separate the opposites by identifying the narrator, in each case, with the "positive" term and "the Jews" with the "negative" term. For the modern reader, however, the narrator's one-sided identification with the world above seems pretentious, not to say farcical. The resistant reader is free to identify, contrary to the author's intention, with Nicodemus, who escapes the one-sidedness of the Evangelist by acknowledging the contradiction (v. 9: "how can these things be?") and by holding the tension. The rational incompatibility of the opposites leads the reader to draw out of the depths of the unconscious a *tertium quid*, as yet unknown.

TEXTS OF PLEASURE/TEXTS OF BLISS

ALTHOUGH THE SOURCE of the energy with which we experience literature is emotional,[159] literary criticism is primarily interested in the cognitive effects of reading, such as "having one's expectations proved false, struggling with an irresolvable ambiguity, or questioning the assumptions on which one had relied."[160] But since spiritual transformation is rarely effected without the involvement of the emotions, biblical empirics must include such psychological symptoms as "feeling shivers along the spine, weeping in sympathy, or being transported in awe."[161] These are precisely the reactions which are wont to result from an encounter with the Holy.

Barthes distinguishes between two kinds of texts: a text of pleasure "comes from culture and does not break with it," whereas a text of bliss "unsettles the reader's historical, cultural and

---

159. Appleyard, *Becoming a Reader,* 39.
160. Culler, *Deconstruction,* 39.
161. Ibid.

psychological assumptions. . . ."[162] Barthes declares that "pleasure can be expressed in words, bliss cannot";[163] he speaks of the "proximity (identity?) of bliss and fear."[164]

Although Barthes makes no explicit mention of the Bible, he does observe that bliss "can erupt, across the centuries, out of certain texts that were nonetheless written to the glory of the dreariest, of the most sinister philosophy."[165]

In a text of pleasure our avidity for knowledge impels us to skim, in order to get more quickly to whatever furthers the solution of the riddle and the revelation of fate.[166] Other texts become opaque and inaccessible to pleasure when read fast. We are captivated not by "the winnowing out of truths, but the layering of significance."[167] The object is "not to devour, to gobble, but to graze, to browse scrupulously."[168] Cryptic texts (like Mark's Gospel?) elicit responses of "shock, disturbance, even loss."[169]

For those who are very familiar with the Bible an avidity for knowledge is no longer possible. The Bible may then be read like a tragedy: "I take pleasure in hearing myself tell a story *whose end I know:* I know and I don't know.[170]" Is the mysterious influence of the vertical axis responsible for this paradox?

SONIA, RASKOLNIKOV, AND THE RESURRECTION OF LAZARUS

AN EXAMPLE IN modern literature of scripture's power to stir the emotions and thus to affect the plot of human lives is found in the scene from Fyodor Dostoevsky's *Crime and Punishment*[171] between the murderer Raskolnikov and the prostitute Sonia. Seeing a

---

162. Barthes, *Pleasure of the Text,* 14.
163. Ibid., 21.
164. Ibid., 48.
165. Ibid., 39.
166. Ibid., 11.
167. Ibid., 12.
168. Ibid., 13.
169. Ibid., 19.
170. Ibid., 47.
171. Fyodor Dostoevsky, *Crime and Punishment,* trans. Constance Garnett (New York: Random House, 1956).

copy of a Russian New Testament in her room, he asks where she got it, and when he learns that it was from one of the women whom he had killed, he suddenly asks her to read him the story of Lazarus, with the startling words, "I shall be a religious maniac myself soon! It's infectious!"[172]

Despite his evident lack of religious belief, Sonia begins to read the eleventh chapter of St. John's Gospel. She does so with difficulty, and Raskolnikov

> understood only too well how painful it was for her to betray and unveil all that was her *own.* He understood that these feelings really were her *secret treasure,* which she had kept perhaps for years, perhaps from childhood, while she lived with an unhappy father and a distracted stepmother crazed by grief, in the midst of starving children and unseemly abuse and reproaches. But at the same time he knew now and knew for certain that, although it filled her with dread and suffering, yet she had a tormenting desire to read and to read to *him* that he might hear it, and to read *now* whatever might come of it.[173]

PRACTICAL COMMUNICATION AND BIBLICAL LITERATURE

BIBLICAL LITERATURE MAY be broadly described as religious propaganda, and its primary genre is therefore "oratorical," as Frye has stated. Biblical rhetoric raises the difficult problem of the pragmatic status of literary utterances.[174] Just as it is necessary to distinguish between the effect of a practical spoken communication, such as "Please shut the window," and the effect of telling a parable, so too it is necessary to distinguish the pragmatics of practical written communication from that of a literary work.

If, for example, I am writing to a colleague to express my interest in a job opening, I will transmit my message by means

---

172. Ibid., 294.

173. Ibid., 295.

174. T. A. van Dijk, "Pragmatics and Poetics" in *The Pragmatics of Language and Literature,* ed. T. A. van Dijk (North Holland Publishing Company, 1976), 23–57.

of a semiotic system, i.e., a natural language, and, perhaps, a system of literary conventions as well. I know or believe that my colleague is familiar with the specific literary system, for only if we both know the rules of language and the conventions used in such a letter can my message be understood. By means of this letter, I intend to change the internal system of my colleague in accordance with my intentions, and I can only hope to do this if my letter is such that my colleague is able to infer correctly what my intentions are.

The success of a literary work, on the contrary, does not depend on the reader's ability to infer the intention of the author. "To understand a text is not to ask 'what was being said in what was said?'"[175] There is no need for the author to express his or her intention, and, if he or she chooses to do so, this need not inhibit the reader.

Neither may it be assumed that the work conveys semantic information, as in the case of my letter to a colleague. Literary messages have traditionally been held to have some form of "symbolic" content, which may lead to further possibilities for interpretation. Within the range of possible interpretations, determined by the constraints of the text, the reader may freely choose those which he or she prefers, i.e., those "truths" which obtain in the worlds accessible to the reader.

According to the logic of actions, the change intended by means of an act of communication is always envisaged in a given state of affairs, i.e., a particular situation occurring at a particular time. In written (indirect) communication, there is usually only a short lapse of time between the production and perception events. But what if persons other than those to whom a communication was written read and interpret it, after an interval of many centuries, in a vastly different cultural situation, and (in the event of translation) in a different language? Then the pragmatic effect is drastically altered, since what was originally a work of religious propaganda has now become a work of literature, in which no systematic reference is made to a "here" and "now" of the utterance act. Since no practical

175. Culler, *Structuralist Poetics,* 30.

interaction in the actual world between writer and reader is possible, the work takes on the disinterested quality characteristic of artistic works (*ars gratia artis*).

THE OBSCURITY OF NARRATIVE

THIS PHENOMENON CAN be illustrated by the obscurity which is characteristic of all narratives and contributes to their hermeneutic potential. The pragmatic effect of obscurity in a written text is the same whether this obscurity is the result of the factors mentioned above or of the creative artistry of the author.

A modern poet like T. S. Eliot may supply notes to *The Waste Land,* and a historical critic may "clear up" the obscurity of ancient texts with explanations of his or her own. But, in either case, we have the impression of unassimilated material which, however interesting and informative, has not been integrated into the verbal symbol of the literary work.

In a spoken parable, the pragmatic effect does not follow from the semantic structure: the referent must be supplied from the system of beliefs and concepts held by the perceiver. A modern reader may recognize him- or herself and his or her own situation in a biblical narrative, but the practical consequence of such an insight may be quite different from what the original readers might have experienced.

The lack of mutual accessibility of the worlds of the writer and the worlds of the reader reduces the set of possible presuppositions; as a result, the message transmitted by the ancient text becomes impersonal. The pragmatic effect can no longer be restricted to what *should* be known, valued, or striven for by a receiver. There are no "shoulds" in literary interpretation.

READING AND VALUE

READING LITERATURE IS "an exploration of the possibilities of experience, a questioning and deepening of the categories in and through which we ordinarily view ourselves and the world."[176] Attention is

---

176. Culler, *Saussure,* 105.

directed not so much to what is said ("semantic" information) as to how it is said ("structural" or "formal" information). The text thus acquires "object" character, with an assigned "value" which depends on the esthetic pleasure, emotional catharsis, or personal insight and transformation which it produces in the reader. "*The Pragmatic Reader* . . . may read in several ways . . .: to escape, to judge the truth of experience, to gratify a sense of beauty, to challenge oneself with new experiences, to comfort oneself with images of wisdom."[177]

Language, Literature, and the Bible

ALTHOUGH MANY COLLEGE courses were being offered on "The Bible *as* Literature" when Northrop Frye wrote *The Great Code,* he quite deliberately used in his subtitle the coordinating, rather than the subordinating, conjunction: *The Bible and Literature.* Helpful as the insights of a distinguished literary critic may be in biblical interpretation, contemporary approaches to literature cannot be imposed on readers of the Bible, and any such attempt would be counterproductive.

What the experience of reading literature does show us is that the meaningfulness of texts does not depend on their being read historically or referentially. Although a text can be read "centrifugally," in order to discover a "fact" (past or present), a metaphysical claim, or the intention of the author, a text can also be read "centripetally, " i.e., as "a verbal structure existing for its own sake."[178] Religious texts in particular can function as "transitional objects" (D. W. Winnicott). The Bible is neither wholly "outside" nor wholly "inside" the reader and thus provides an intermediate area of experience where inner and outer are fused.[179] This intense experiencing, which is characteristic of imaginative living, offers us an alternative to the logocentric perspective which dominates both historico-critical and doctrinal approaches to the Bible. The written word need not be used exclusively as a means to uncover what the writer had in mind.

---

177. Appleyard, *Becoming a Reader,* 15.
178. Frye, *The Great Code,* 57.
179. Appleyard, *Becoming a Reader,* 55.

Literature, like language, is rule-governed creativity, but the rules in each case are quite different. A linguist could tell us, without much difficulty, why a particular English utterance is incorrect, i.e., which rule of English grammar or usage has been violated. A literary critic seeks to understand the conventions which make literature possible,[180] but these conventions cannot be elucidated in the same way as the rules of a language.

> [I]f there were a straightforward and explicit semiotic code which provided an automatic interpretation for every literary work, literature would be of much less interest, and the first thing authors would do is to violate or go beyond the rules of this code.[181]

Consequently, linguistic competence (e.g., the ability to read English) and literary competence (the ability to make sense of literary texts) are quite different. For if there is no explicit code which provides an interpretation for a literary work, then it is not possible to say that a literary interpretation is right or wrong, at least not with the same assurance with which one can say that an English utterance is correct or incorrect.

Biblical empirics also has to do with creativity, since it brings about what in religious terminology is called "a new creation" (2 Cor. 5:17; Gal. 6:15). But this creativity is not governed by the same rules as language or literature. The transformation effected by reading the Bible is the work of the spirit, and the spirit's appearance is unpredictable, like the wind, which "blows where it will" (John 3:8). The spirit is

> an archetypal image of a primordial human experience of assistance from a power that transcends our ordinary resources. Whether we explain that power as parental or divine or as a personification of the highest capacities of our own psyches, on the level of archetype we experience it as the spirit spontaneously manifesting itself and supplying what is needed for a psychic integration that we are at the moment incapable of achieving by ourselves.[182]

---

180. Culler, *Structuralist Poetics,* viii.
181. Culler, *Saussure,* 114.
182. Appleyard, *Becoming a Reader,* 43.

Moreover, in biblical empirics the emphasis is on the *effects of reading*; the text serves as a catalyst for an experience which changes the reader. Undoubtedly there are many passages in scripture which merit being considered literary masterpieces, but it is quite possible for a reader to be profoundly moved and deeply changed by a text which could never aspire to such a status. Recall Barthes's comment about the "bliss" occasioned by reading a "dreary" text. Such effects, though unpredictable and disproportionate to the literary quality of the text which occasioned them, are not necessarily arbitrary, as the following two chapters will seek to elucidate.

LITERATURE AND PSYCHOLOGY

MODERN LITERARY CRITICISM considers diversity in interpretation to be not a difficulty but a given, one which presents the critic with the challenge of explaining how the unchanging text can generate an almost infinite series of variant readings. Biblical empirics also regards different responses to the text as a given, but since emotional responses, not normally the concern of literary criticism, are included in biblical empirics, it is necessary to go beyond the semantic level in addressing the question of how these responses have come about.

As we have seen, literary critics are divided on the question whether "subjective" reactions to literature have any rightful place in the work of interpretation. Supporters of "the autonomous text" would respond with a strong negative, whereas one school of reader response criticism would respond affirmatively. But literary critics, almost by definition, are oriented to texts; they leave it to psychologists to study the psychic origin of the images of which the literary artist has made use.

The Jungian analyst Joseph Henderson affirms, "The artist is not merely a mouthpiece for the unconscious."[183] Henderson analyzed many artists, including Jackson Pollack, and he was acutely aware of the dangers inherent in confusing artistic and

---

183. Joseph Henderson, "The Artist's Relation to the Unconscious" in Sugg, *Jungian Literary Criticism,* 54.

psychological development. The therapeutic process and the artistic process are distinct, and the latter should not be reduced to the former.

The artist's image is the "outward innermost" source of inspiration (Joseph Campbell).[184] Artistic creativity is engendered through "an enchantment of the heart": "An object apparently without passes into the soul forever, and the soul leaps to the call." (James Joyce)[185] The vitality of any work of art comes from the complex interplay of the artist's own variables within his or her own artistic intent, and the literary critic's analysis of the work cannot be made dependent on a psychological theory.

For biblical empirics the primary thing is not the artistic work, or whether or not the Bible qualifies to be considered such, but the transformation of consciousness for which the Bible serves as a catalyst. Consequently, our concern is not the competence of the artist or of the critic but the competence of the reader whose life is changed by reading the Bible.

Today those who read the Bible do not normally know the linguistic codes used by the biblical authors, and their access to the text is through vernacular translations. (The New Testament writers were in the same situation with respect to the Hebrew Bible.) Where knowledge of the *linguistic* codes used in the original text cannot be presupposed, it seems gratuitous to demand of the contemporary reader a knowledge of the *semantic* codes which may have been shared by the authors and their original readers. In the case of this very special book, those who are affected by reading it thereby demonstrate their interpretative competence.

Art and therapy should not be confused, and it is obvious that for biblical empirics the therapeutic effect of Bible reading is more important than the book's artistic status. Consequently, we will conclude our consideration of language and literature and proceed to a consideration of the psyche or soul, where language and literature originate and where religious transformation takes place. Here the "rule governed creativity" of language and literature gives way to the new creation brought about by the spirit.

---

184. Quoted in Henderson, "Artist's Relation," 57.
185. Ibid.

3. The Mysterious Revelation

Deep calls to deep.

—Ps. 42:7

C. G. JUNG DID not consider himself competent in literary criticism,[186] and he died before reader response criticism appeared on the scene. Nevertheless, his own reading of scripture, as illustrated in *Answer to Job,* is an excellent example of reader-oriented interpretation. In particular, Jung exemplifies what I have called "biblical empirics." He writes:

> Since I shall be dealing with numinous factors, my feeling is challenged quite as much as my intellect. I cannot, therefore, write in a coolly objective manner, but must allow my emotional subjectivity to speak if I want to describe what I feel when I read certain books of the Bible. . . .[187] I shall not give a cool and carefully considered exegesis that tries to be fair to every detail, but a purely subjective reaction.[188]

The theologian and the historian—and even the literary critic —may wonder what to make of such an encounter with the biblical text. Nevertheless, this type of reaction to scripture, for which Jung provides a particularly clear example, cannot be dismissed or ignored. The Christian faith holds out a promise of new life and personal transformation, and scripture has frequently served as the vehicle for such transformation, whether it be that of a dramatic conversion, or, less dramatically, the gradual spiritual growth which takes place over the course of a lifetime. In

---

186. Jung, *CW,* vol. 11, 311.
187. Ibid., 363.
188. Ibid., 365.

such experiences we are brought face to face with the creative sources of our existence and discover the deepest meanings of our lives. Now such an experience is rarely, if ever, a purely rational matter. (The Greek word *metanoia*, commonly translated "repentance," is not simply a "change of mind" but a reorientation of the entire personality, as the Hebrew equivalent *shub* ["turn"] suggests.)

To be changed means to be "moved," and to be "moved" involves the emotions. The reader who experiences the transformative reality which is mediated by the scriptural text cannot help being touched emotionally. Indeed, it is not uncommon for the reading or hearing of scripture to result in tears or uncontrollable sobbing. This emotional impact of scripture may occur prior to any interpretation of the text. Interpretation is a deliberate, reflective act, but the emotional response wells up spontaneously within the reader from a deep level of the psyche. An interpreter tries to "make sense" out of a text, but when we are deeply moved by scripture, we are responding to something which we have not "made;" we are not acting but being acted upon. Something in the text has elicited feelings of enlargement, union, or emancipation which may have no specific intellectual content.[189] This experience comes about not through discursive reasoning but through an intuitive sense which penetrates the darkness where God is (Exod. 20:21).

BEYOND HERMENEUTICS

IF WE ARE to attempt to understand what is going on in such a reading situation, we cannot remain within the framework of conventional hermeneutics or semantics. In the chapter on literary criticism we noted the phenomenon of "misreadings," which ignore or contradict the "clear" guidelines for interpretation which the critic finds in the text. Plurivocity always seems to characterize textual interpretation. The varied response to the biblical text attested in the history of interpretation cannot be explained by the rules of semantics, and when the emotions are involved,

---

189. James, *Varieties of Religious Experience,* 410.

the unpredictability is even greater. The indeterminacy of biblical empirics brings us close to the kind of appreciation and
response which is typical of art, music, and poetry.

These types of human creativity do not reveal their secrets to
rational analysis but engage the "irrational" functions of feeling
and intuition. The "meaning" of a poem or symphony cannot be
formulated in conceptual language. Although the formal *structure*
of the work may be elucidated by rational analysis, the whole is
more than the sum of the parts, and either you "get" it or you
don't. What is true of artistic experience is also true of interpersonal relations. Knowing another person is quite different from
knowing *about* another person.

Directed and Fantasy Thinking

THOSE STUDYING THE Bible from theological and historical per-
spectives regard scripture as "[h]ypostatized content, invariable
and discoverable."[190] They analyze this content in accordance
with what Jung has called "directed" or logical thinking.[191] Such
thinking is adapted to reality; it takes for granted the principle of
contradiction, and it imitates the causal sequence of events taking
place outside the mind. Directed thinking analyzes the thought of
a biblical author and reconstructs the historical situation which a
biblical book is thought to reflect. In directed thinking the emotional response of a reader is completely irrelevant.

For biblical empirics, however, the Bible is viewed not as content but as catalyst, i.e., a means of bringing the reader into
contact with something beyond his or her control, something
which Jung, following Rudolf Otto, called the *numinosum*: an awe-
inspiring manifestation which touches us and shakes us to the
core, regardless of whether or not we understand it.[192] Something
arises out of the depths which is beyond the reach of personal
caprice, something which we experience as a revelation.

---

190. Stephen Moore, *Literary Criticism and the Gospels* (New Haven:
Yale University Press, 1989), 66.

191. Jung, *CW,* vol. 5, 18.

192. E. C. Whitmont, *The Symbolic Quest* (Princeton, N.J.: Princeton
University Press, 1978), 83.

Susceptibility to such influences is regarded with deep suspicion in our highly rationalistic society. Jung has argued that during the second millennium of the Christian era a myth of rationality has taken hold that effectively excludes the perception of the divine. Even mainline Christianity is leery of anything bordering on "enthusiasm" (literally, "possession by a god"), and psychology itself is disposed to regard such manifestations as pathological. Thinking and sensation are the faculties by which we relate to the external world and seek to bring it under our control. Concepts have tended to replace images in Western society.

Biblical empirics involves fantasy thinking which, unlike directed thinking, works spontaneously and is guided by unconscious motives. Fantasy thinking sets free subjective tendencies, and rather than adapting itself to reality, instead adapts external reality to its own inner world. Contradictions abound, as our own dreams testify every night. In Freudian terms, fantasy thinking is primary process thinking; directed thinking is secondary process thinking.

THE LOSS OF THE IMAGE

JUNG BELIEVED THAT modern men and women have forgotten how to experience reality symbolically, and he was convinced that our separation from the imagistic approach to experience puts us in great danger. The emphasis on rational thought has crowded out any other way of responding to the world or the text. (Modern literary theory emphasizes the parallelism between these two sources of experience.) Jung believed that both directed and fantasy thinking are essential for successful human functioning, and he rejected the devaluation of the image as inferior. To be sure, the inability to relate to the external world through directed thinking is characteristic of a psychotic personality. But the inner world has its own reality, and it is impossible to relate to this world without the use of fantasy, image, and symbol. Fantasy thinking is an essential compensation for the rational, directed thinking which characterizes our life in the external world. A one-sided emphasis on the type of thinking which we need for getting on in "the real world" makes us incapable of experiencing reality symbolically.

This problem is at the root of much contemporary neurosis. For the practical utilization of external things does not satisfy the deepest longings of the human heart. Everything which makes life truly worth living depends on foundations which elude rational analysis, and therefore, as Jung observes, "the more critical reason dominates, the more impoverished life becomes."[193] The functions of feeling and intuition, by which we relate to factors beyond our control or even our understanding, are indispensable for a fully human existence, and these are precisely the functions which are involved in biblical empirics. Our attention shifts from a consideration of the text as an expression of directed thinking to an experience of the archetypal world which the text reflects. Biblical empirics is an important complement to the rational modes of doctrinal construction and historical reconstruction which are the predominant approaches to the biblical text.

LECTIO DIVINA

THE RATIONAL DISSECTION of the biblical text (whether from a theological, a historical, or a literary perspective) needs to be balanced by an approach which examines and respects another property of this same text: its ability to engage the reader's emotions and thus to produce human transformation. The transformative power of such a reading gives it significance, quite apart from whatever textual meaning may be generated in the process. The private reading of scripture, which allows for personal and emotional reactions, has always coexisted, under the name of *lectio divina*, with the church's doctrinal reading of scripture. It still has an important place in monastic life, and it is an essential part of the spiritual life of any committed Christian.

Jung, following Tertullian, believed that "the statements made in the Holy Scriptures are also utterances of the soul."[194] The world of religious ideas is based on "an emotional foundation which is unassailable by reason."[195] Jung thus reclaims for theology the dimension

---

193. Jung, *Memories, Dreams, Reflections*, 333.
194. Jung, *CW*, vol. 11, 362.
195. Ibid., 361.

described by Pseudo-Dionysius as "experiencing divine things" (*pathôn ta theia*). Jung was a physician and a man of science, and he accepted the empirical assumptions of the scientific tradition. However, he extended "experience" to include not only observable phenomena in the outside world but also inner experience, which is every bit as real. The world of inner experience, to which biblical empirics belongs, is an essential part of what it means to be human, and giving it due attention is healthy, not pathological. Such inner reality is "something that always demonstrates itself and is experienced on its own merits."[196] To be sure, Jung distinguished between the "psychic effects" of religious experience and their "metaphysical background," which he, in keeping with the apophatic mystical tradition, considered "unknowable."[197]

BIBLICAL EMPIRICS AS AN ACT OF GOD

BUT WHAT IS it about the text which produces such effects? Before the inroads of Enlightenment thinking, one could refer to scripture unhesitatingly as an instrument of God's spirit and a product of divine inspiration. Commenting on the sudden changes of mood which we have been considering, Ignatius of Loyola declares:

> It belongs to God alone to give consolation to the soul without previous cause . . . , that is, without any previous perception or knowledge of any object from which consolation might come to the soul through its own acts of intellect and will.[198]

Such language is more congruent with the structure of the psyche than "rational" explanations, which all too frequently alienate us from the experience which we are attempting to explain. In Jung's words,

> It is not a matter of indifference whether one calls something a "mania" or a "god." To serve a mania is detestable and undignified, but to serve a god is full of meaning and promise

196. Ibid., 360.
197. Ibid., 363.
198. Ignatius, *Spiritual Exercises,* 133.

because it is an act of submission to a higher, invisible, and spiritual being. . . .[199]

JUNG'S THEORY OF THE ARCHETYPES

BUT ALTHOUGH THE terms "inspiration" and "consolation" remain intelligible within the world of theological discourse, they pose a problem when we are attempting to explain the phenomenon in question to a broader audience. That is why we appeal, in this chapter, to Jung's theory of the archetypes. Although we are not undertaking to "prove" anything, every approach to interpretation requires a theory,[200] and biblical empirics is no exception. It is important to stress at the outset, that Jung's theory of the archetypes is *only* a theory, "which can be exchanged at any time for a better formula."[201] It is simply a model which helps us understand why reading scripture produces certain effects which might otherwise be regarded as unworthy of serious consideration; it is not a metaphysical postulate nor does it compete with the explanations of faith.

In all literature there are certain universal motifs which have persisted throughout recorded history with very little change. Because of their strong feeling tone they have the power to impress, influence, and fascinate us. Such "archetypal" imagery has been studied by Northrop Frye, who, toward the end of his life, turned his attention to the Bible in works entitled *The Great Code* (1982) and *Words with Power* (1990). Frye writes of archetypal imagery in the following terms:

> Patterns of imagery . . . , or fragments of significance, are oracular in origin, and derive from the epiphanic moment, the flash of instantaneous comprehension with no direct reference to

---

199. Jung, *CW,* vol. 13, 38.

200. There is no possibility of escaping theory, since the escape routes themselves are paved with theory. Those who claim simply to declare "what the Bible says" need to reflect on their own unexpressed, unexamined, and probably unconscious presuppositions.

201. Jung, *CW,* vol. 11, 306.

> time. . . . The myth is the central informing power that gives archetypal significance to the ritual and archetypal narrative to the oracle.[202]

The conscious use of archetypal imagery by a writer is the concern of literary criticism, for which symbols and images are the raw material used in the work of art, the "building blocks" employed by the creative genius of the artist. Although we have no reason to exclude such a concern from the study of scripture, the effect of archetypal imagery upon the feeling and intuition of the reader of the Bible need not be the result of the sacred author's conscious literary intent. Indeed, since scripture, broadly speaking, can be classified as religious propaganda, its effect upon feeling and intuition is more likely to be unintended than deliberate. It is the result not of the intention of the author but of the archetypal nature of religious language itself. The rhetoric represents the surface structure of the text; beneath the rhetoric lies the deep structure of an archetypal world out of which the text has arisen and which it is still capable of reflecting.

One could compare the contrast which Richard Wagner makes between the vocal line and the orchestra:

> There [in the orchestra] the primal urge of creation and nature are represented. What the orchestra expresses can never be clearly articulated, because it renders primal feeling itself. . . . No wonder that when we are first exposed to Wagner our attention goes to the orchestra. It puts us in touch with the very depths of our unconscious feelings.[203]

Jung traced the origin of archetypal imagery to irrepresentible, unconscious, pre-existent forms which are part of the inherited structure of the psyche. These forms govern the functioning of our imagination in a way analogous to the way in which the instincts govern our biological functioning. Like Immanuel Kant's forms of apperception, the archetypes are unknowable in themselves. Jung

---

202. Northrop Frye, "The Archetypes of Literature" in Sugg, *Jungian Literary Criticism,* 23.

203. David Stanley–Porter, "The Fascination with 'Tristan und Isolde,'" *Canadian Opera Company Magazine* (Sept.–Oct. 1987), 39.

compared the form of an archetype to the axial system of a crystal, which preforms the crystalline structure in the mother liquid, although it has no material existence of its own.[204] "The archetypes are as it were the hidden foundations of the conscious mind . . . , systems of readiness for action . . . , images and emotions."[205] Though without any existence of their own, they make possible all specifically human types of experience, such as the visualizations which we call archetypal images. These images are therefore by no means random or arbitrary but come from a psychic predisposition beyond time and space, which explains their numinous effect.

THE ROLE OF THE ARCHETYPES IN HUMAN EXPERIENCE

JUNG SEES THE archetypes as exercising the same role in relation to our specifically human functioning which the instincts exercise in relation to our biological functioning. As instincts, the archetypes are unknowable in themselves. They are inferred from the effects which they produce. They are, as it were, the "wiring" by which we have a capacity for specifically human actions and perceptions. Jung rejected Freud's limitation of libido to sexuality and understood psychic energy to include our spiritual drives.[206] The archetypes are located at the interface between the individual and collective aspects of our psychology. On the one hand, they are the result of a process of human development which has gone on since the beginning of our race. On the other hand, they activate our very personal complexes, those highly charged, nonrational patterns of feeling and behavior, grouped around certain emotions and ideas, which function like fragmentary personalities.

The world of the text and the world of the psyche are two paths which are destined to intersect, as the key is made for the lock; the energy transfer between the two worlds comes about, in Jung's theory, through the agency of the archetypes. The archetypal imagery of the text corresponds to the archetypal basis of the complexes of the reader. But it is only because the archetype

---

204. Jung, *CW,* vol. 9, pt. 1, 79.
205. Ibid., vol. 10, 31.
206. Ibid., vol. 5, 132–41.

includes both the image and the instinctual emotion that it is able to effect the energy transfer to the psyche of the reader.

ARCHETYPAL ENERGY AND MORALITY

SINCE ARCHETYPAL ENERGY is of an instinctual nature, it is neither good nor bad; it simply is. How it is used and where it leads is the responsibility of the individual, who will try to channel this energy within his or her personal value system. Archetypal energy might be compared to the gasoline in a car. It does not determine where the car will go, but without it the car won't go anywhere. Similarly, the archetypes do not impose the direction or pace of psychic growth, but they provide the momentum without which growth is impossible. Jung believed that everything in nature, whether a yucca moth or a human being, has an innate drive towards completion—not perfection, i.e., to become what it is. What is true in the external world is also true in the psyche: "Mother nature will find a way over, under or around anything you put in its path."[207]

If human beings are made in the image and likeness of God (Gen. 1:26), then the drive towards completion has an infinite goal and is only partially attainable in this life. However, progress toward that goal is the measure of successful human existence. It is important to note that Jung calls this process "individuation." It is the individual who is to be transformed through the transfer of archetypal energy, and the individual must retain responsibility for this transformation.

To be sure, the ego must suffer defeat in recognizing that it is not sole master in its own house. Nevertheless, if the ego surrenders entirely, the individual is flooded by contents from the unconscious, and psychosis is the result. There is a paradoxical tension between "letting go" and "holding on."

Without moral responsibility nothing good can happen. In a collective situation, where a mob suspends all sense of individual responsibility and surrenders to a demagogue, archetypal energies can be manipulated for destructive and diabolical ends. Jung witnessed two examples of such "psychic infection": Fascism and

---

207. *Time,* May 5, 1997, 19.

Bolshevism.[208] He noted how archetypal and religious symbolism can be used in the service of an all-powerful state. Even if the collective experience results in nothing more sinister than mass hysteria, there is no lasting psychic gain. True inner progress is only available on an individual basis.

THE ARCHETYPAL READING OF SCRIPTURE

ARCHETYPAL EXEGESIS RESTS on the conviction that the structure of the inner world has a universal character. Like the *a priori* categories of Kant, the archetypes are universal inherited possibilities. Like biological instincts, they "direct all fantasy activity into its appointed paths."[209] But these *a priori* norms of psychic activity only take on existence in concrete, individual images, and, within a religious tradition, these images undergo a cultural process, which transforms them into a symbol system of collective consciousness.

Archetypal reading is introverted: it understands the text to be the *mimesis* of the psychic processes which produced it, and it listens for resonances which the reading of the text produces in the psyche of the reader ("heart speaks to heart"). Archetypal interpretation is avowedly subjective, but it is not solipsistic. It attempts to formulate and to communicate the reading experience, while inviting others to share our experience of the text, which serves as a prism between the numinous world behind the text and the psyche of the reader.

If reading scripture may be compared to a discussion between two people, then Jung's conversation with the Book of Job is not the "objective" discussion of the theologian or the historical critic. The Book of Job constellated complexes in Jung as reader—complexes which assimilated whatever might have been under rational discussion in the text.

Jung himself says that he dealt with the problem posed by the story of Job

---

208. For the context of Jung's ill-timed comparison between the Jewish and "Aryan" unconscious, see Stein, *Jung's Treatment of Christianity*, 85–87.

209. Jung, *CW*, vol. 9, pt. 1, 66.

in the form of describing a personal experience, carried by subjective emotions. I deliberately chose this form because I wanted
to avoid the impression that I had any idea of announcing an
"eternal truth."[210]

When scripture is read in this way, the "intention" of the biblical
author is frustrated, and answers related to the reader's complexes are elicited by the archetypal forces at work in the text.
Psychoanalysis provides an illuminating analogy for this process:
real progress only occurs when the unconscious of the analyst
interacts with the unconscious of the client; discussion at the level
of ego consciousness alone rarely leads to significant change.

THE EXPERIENCE OF THE ARCHETYPAL WORLD

ALTHOUGH THE DISCOVERY of the unconscious is a modern
development, it is hard not to think of unconscious influence
when Ignatius speaks of psychic changes which come about
"without any previous perception or knowledge of any object . . .
through its [the soul's] own acts of intellect or will."[211] If modern
psychology speaks of the unconscious where earlier ages spoke of
God, this may be, as Jung suggests, "because God has in fact
become unconscious to us."[212]

Although the archetypes are innate, archetypal images first
enter consciousness through the principal figures in the child's
life, usually the father and mother. The personal shortcomings of
these key figures, who are "larger than life" to the child whom
they are influencing, result in the archetypes becoming conscious
in a truncated or distorted form. Once the child has separated
from the family situation, there is a need for the picture to be
completed by filling in those aspects of the archetypal world
which were not represented in the childhood experience.

The highly charged, nonrational patterns of feeling and behavior called complexes have two aspects: a shell and a core.[213] The

---

210. Jung, *CW,* vol. 11, 358.
211. Ignatius, *Spiritual Exercises,* 133.
212. Jung, *CW,* vol. 11, 320.
213. Whitmont, *Symbolic Quest,* 65.

shell is the peculiar reaction pattern which has been individually acquired through a network of associations. For example, if a person's father has been a harsh disciplinarian, the result may be a father complex which nurtures resentment towards any expression of authority. The *core* of the complex, in Jung's view, is mythological and consists of a universal or "archetypal" human pattern. The eternal mythological motif is incarnated in the personal shell of the complex.

To understand the causes for one's personal complexes and to attempt to sublimate them constitute the limits of conventional psychotherapy. But for Jung such conscious striving falls far short of what is possible through a transformation of the core of the complex: a redirection of the emotional energy associated with the complex in a positive direction. Then this energy ceases to be a disturbing intruder which thwarts our conscious purposes. The personal conflict is understood in relation to a perennial theme, e.g., the need for deliverance from "the father," now understood as a dominant principle of consciousness which is no longer adequate for the son.[214] If the personal problem can be experienced in this way, the conscious mind is no longer obsessed by it, and the energy associated with it becomes a constructive and helpful impulse. The traditional Christian practice of associating our personal sufferings with those of Christ on the cross is an example of such archetypal transformation.

Progressive psychic transformation through the assimilation of archetypal energy corrects the one-sidedness which was the inevitable outcome of our efforts to establish ourselves in the external world. Particularly in the latter half of life we experience, especially through dreams, transpersonal messages of what yet needs to be done if the uniqueness with which each of us has been graced is to reach fulfilment. Although the Bible is full of dreams, it rarely occurs to religious people today to consider *their* dreams as revelatory. But if they regard the *Bible* as a source of revelation, then the archetypal images which *it* contains can further the work of spiritual transformation.

---

214. Ibid., 71.

ARCHETYPAL IMAGES AS SYMBOLIC

THE PROBLEM IS that these images are symbolic. A genuine symbol, in Jung's view, is "the expression of a spontaneous experience which points beyond itself to a meaning not conveyed by a rational term,"[215] since the rational term is intrinsically limited. A symbol is "the best description, or formulation, of a relatively unknown fact; which is nonetheless known to exist or is postulated as existing."[216]

Symbols work, in Jung's view, because there is something unknown in the symbol which corresponds to something unknown in the perceiver. "Mystical participation" (Lucien Lévy–Bruhl) is characteristic of symbols, since a symbol always includes the unconscious, within which the individual too is contained.[217] The numinosity of the symbol is an expression of this fact. Learning to value these symbolic messages and to interpret their meaning is a lifelong task, one which is rendered more difficult by the blindness to symbolic reality of our rationalistic culture. Symbols are paradoxical and ambiguous; they unite opposites which do not go together in our everyday experience. We are therefore tempted to dismiss them as contradictory and nonsensical. But once a symbol has been explained, it is no longer a symbol. It has become a sign for something which can be adequately expressed in conceptual terms (e.g., red = "stop!").

THE "MORE" OF RELIGIOUS EXPERIENCE

ALL RELIGIONS CLAIM to offer their adherents something which is higher, better, and purer than what we experience in the ordinary course of our everyday lives. The Johannine Jesus said, "I have come that they may have life and have it more abundantly" (John 10:10). Psychology in general, and Jungian psychology in particular, recognizes that there is more in our inner life than we are aware of at any time. J. A. Sanford has stated:

---

215. Ibid., 18.
216. Jung, *CW,* vol. 6, 474.
217. Ibid., vol. 11, 221n.

The discovery of the reality of the inner world [of the uncon-scious]—of which we are ordinarily unaware but which greatly affects our conscious life—is the most important religious fact of our time.[218]

William James suggests that the "more" of religious experience may be considered to be the subconscious continuation of our conscious life:

the theologian's contention that the religious man is moved by an external power is vindicated, for it is one of the pecu-liarities of invasions from the subconscious region to take on objective appearances, and to suggest to the Subject an exter-nal control. . . .[219]

Jung believed that the autonomous psychic contents which intrude upon our consciousness without our will, or even against it, are more just than repressed personal material. In dreams we expe-rience images which go beyond our personal experience and there-fore point to a transpersonal origin. A transpersonal factor would also seem to be involved when the reading of scripture leads to psy-chic changes which are not the result of conscious acts on our part.

ARCHETYPAL IMAGERY IN THE BIBLE

WHAT IS THE function of archetypal imagery in religious litera-ture? Among the various images which fascinate and frighten us there are some which might be called images of wholeness. They represent symbolically the totality from which we come and of which we are a part. For Jung, the cross was such a symbol, representing in its four points the four directions (up–down, right–left) or the four corners of the earth. The cross is a simple form of the mandala, a centering device used in Tibetan Buddhism to facilitate concentration during meditation.

In the Old Testament, the bush seen by Moses in the wilderness, which "was burning and yet not consumed" (Exod. 3:2), is such an

---

218. J. A. Sanford, *The Kingdom Within,* rev. ed. (San Francisco: Harper & Row, 1987), 10.

219. James, *Varieties of Religious Experience,* 488.

image of totality, embracing as it does two opposites which, in our everyday experience, do not go together. For Jung, this union of opposites is essential for a true symbol, which expresses something which cannot be expressed in any other way.

The two examples given above (the cross and the burning bush) are both impersonal. Many Christian symbols are personal, but here too we encounter the paradoxical union of opposites: the Virgin Mother, the Crucified Lord, the Word made Flesh. Each of these symbolic images defies rational explanation or analysis and thereby directs the believer to the inconceivable Other, in whom, or in which, all opposites are united.

RELIGIOUS SYMBOLS AND THE DAWN OF CONSCIOUSNESS

THE STORY OF Adam and Eve preserves, in narrative form, the recollection of that defining point at which the human species attained the gift—and curse—of consciousness, by which men and women became able to know good and evil (Gen. 3:5). This power to reflect and discriminate, which, as far as we know, distinguishes human beings from the rest of creation, led to questions which have continued to haunt us ever since: Where have I come from? Why am I here? Where am I going?

The Christian church provides clearly formulated answers to these existential questions:"Man is created to praise, reverence, and serve God our Lord, and by these means to save his soul."[220] But at the dawn of human consciousness it would seem that these questions about our place and purpose in the universe led not to conceptual formulations but to powerful images, such as we find painted in prehistoric caves in France and Spain. In the beginning was the image, not the word. What these images lack in clarity ("What do they *mean?*"), they make up for in emotive power: we are changed by contemplating them.

Christian doctrine is linked to the thinking of antiquity insofar as its subject matter is religious fantasy. This is, perhaps, best appreciated by those outside the religious tradition, who find Christian beliefs "fantastic," precisely because of the union of opposites or "contradictions" which symbolic language inevitably

---

220. Ignatius, *Spiritual Exercises,* 47 ("Principle and Foundation").

entails. But in Christianity's adaptation to the culture of reason, its "fantastic" subject matter is treated dialectically, through directed thinking. In this sense, Christian scholasticism can be called "the mother of our modern scientific method."[221]

An archetypal approach to scripture returns the biblical symbols to the psychic matrix from which they have come and removes the barrier between religion and experience which Jung found to be the greatest weakness of Western religion. We must, however, always keep in mind that

> Even the best attempts at explanation are only more or less successful translations into another metaphorical language. . . .
> The most we can do is *to dream the myth onwards* and give it a modern dress.[222]

221. Jung, *CW,* vol. 5, 20.
222. Ibid., vol. 9, pt. 1, 160.

4. The Alchemy of Language

The letter kills, but the spirit gives life.
—2 Cor. 3:6

RELIGIOUS EXPERIENCE, SCRIPTURE, AND LANGUAGE

RELIGIOUS EXPERIENCE IS mediated in many different ways. The experience received by the mystics, like that received in dreams, is communicated through symbols and images. In some religious traditions, such as Zen Buddhism, written scripture plays a quite subordinate role. However, in all three Abrahamic faiths a scriptural canon is essential. (The burning of the Bible in certain left-wing enthusiastic sects of the Reformation is an exception which proves the rule.)

Our study of "text and psyche" brings us to a consideration of language both as the vehicle by which the biblical text is communicated and as the medium by which it is received. We shall be concerned with the contrast between written and spoken language, as well as with language as the supraindividual system used in communication, of which we are usually unconscious. The foreigner who must first bring to consciousness the rules for formulating a correct sentence before he or she can speak it will never attain fluency in the language.

Jung compared the dream to "an unknown text,"[223] and this comparison supports our move in applying to the workings of the Bible the same process of energy transfer which operates in dream work. Nevertheless, a dream and a text are obviously different: we *see* a dream (or a vision); we *read* a text. In recording a dream we seek to express the dream's imagery in words; in

---

223. Jung, *CW*, vol. 16, 150.

reading the Bible we discover images through interpreting the text. Language is involved in both dreams and texts, but in different ways.

Language has always been a major concern in psychological research, and that is scarcely surprising: we human beings express ourselves in language and are affected by language. The old saying, "Sticks and stones may break my bones, but names can never hurt me," is manifestly untrue. We are the only living creatures who *can* be hurt by words, and this vulnerability to language is an important part of what it means to be human. Moreover, our speech is influenced by unconscious psychic factors, as the phenomenon of "Freudian slips" makes abundantly clear. So language and psyche affect each other reciprocally.

THE ARCHETYPAL DIMENSION OF LANGUAGE

WHAT WE WROTE in the previous chapter about the child's coming into relationship with the archetypal world also applies to language. The unconscious web of linguistic associations, both semantic and phonetic, interacts with emotionally charged patterns of meaning, which lie outside consciousness and which are called complexes. Language studies have shown that a child's brain is definitely not a blank slate. We have an innate capacity for language from birth, but this capacity must be activated by hearing people speak. Frederick II of Sicily's famous experiment in which he attempted to ascertain the original language of humankind did not turn out as he expected: the children whom he left in isolation did not grow up to speak anything. Deprived of human contact, they perished.

Through the unconscious assimilation of a linguistic system, which begins in earliest childhood, "man is separated from the material world (external objects of reference) and initiated into a shared archetypal system of meaning-relations. . . ."[224] Language, as an archetypal reality, stands at the intersection of the psychic and physical worlds and, like the ancient alchemist,

---

224. Paul Kugler, *The Alchemy of Discourse* (Toronto: Associated University Presses, 1982), 117.

seeks to mediate between the two. The Bible, as a transitional object, is related both to the physical world and to the reader.

THE TWO AXES OF LANGUAGE

IN ORDER TO clarify the role of language in both the transmission and the reception of the biblical text, we return to what we said earlier about the two axes of language: the syntactical and the paradigmatic. The syntactical axis, which binds words together, forms a context which limits meaning through the constraints of grammar and syntax. When scholars talk about the "literal" meaning of a word, they are usually referring to the meaning imposed on a word by the context in which it occurs. The syntactical axis is the axis of prose.

The paradigmatic axis joins words together not by grammatical rules but by association. It has been called the axis of poetry, and it corresponds to harmony in music. "Free association" is a technique used to expand the content of dreams. In the development of biblical tradition the paradigmatic axis has played a notable role. Biblical writers and interpreters have frequently been dissatisfied with the "literal" meaning seemingly imposed by syntactical constraints and have sought to find a deeper meaning by a sort of "free association." Paul brings together two completely unrelated texts which "happen" to include the word "reckon":

> Abraham believed God, and it was *reckoned* to him as righteousness (Gen. 15:6).

> Blessed is the man against whom the Lord will not *reckon* his sin (Ps. 32:2).

By joining together these two texts, which have just one word in common, Paul turns the righteous Abraham into the model for the justified sinner, directly contradicting the understanding of Jewish tradition (Rom. 4:1–8).

Similarly, Matthew cites the "virgin" from the Greek text of Isa. 7:14 in his account of the miraculous conception of Jesus (Matt. 1:23). There is nothing miraculous in Isaiah's prophecy: *every* woman who conceives and bears a child has once been a virgin. However, when Mary is found to be with child before she and

Joseph had come together (Matt. 1:18), the suspicion of adultery (or rape) can only be averted by a supernatural explanation: "the holy spirit" (Matt. 1:20). This confers on Isaiah's prophecy a totally new meaning. Matthew's disregard for the "original" context of Isa. 7:14 would be totally unacceptable in a modern interpreter, but for the biblical writer such disregard seems to be the rule, rather than the exception. *For the religious imagination, association is more powerful than grammar.* Language is always figurative and symbolic, and it is futile to try to isolate the "true" lexical sense of a word, particularly in religious discourse.

SEMANTIC AND PHONETIC ASSOCIATION

LINGUISTIC ASSOCIATION CAN be based on either meaning or sound. In Jung's association experiment he discovered that the more the subject's attention was reduced, the more the associations were phonetic (sound-based), rather than semantic (-meaning-based). With increasing unconsciousness the associations are "more and more influenced by sound, till finally only a sound is associated."[225] The linguistic system appears to order meanings through acoustic images of similar sound. The correlation between diminished consciousness and susceptibility to phonetic factors suggests that the energy transfer in biblical empirics has to do not only with visual imagery but also with acoustic images. In some religious traditions great importance is attached to sounds or mantras which have no definable meaning.[226]

To the two types of thinking which we discussed earlier— directed thinking and fantasy thinking—there correspond two different uses of language: communicative and expressive. Communicative language is used in our dealings with the outside world; expressive language touches our hearts and souls. The poetics of the lyric subjects language to a different teleology or finality from that of ordinary speech; its purpose is aesthetic, rather than informational: "[Aesthetic creation] is not, properly

---

225. Jung, *CW*, vol. 2, 171.
226. Harold Coward and David Goa, *Mantra* (Chambersburg, Pa.: Anima Books, 1991).

speaking, communication. . . . In aesthetic creation, the art work
has import in itself. It is not a signal to share information."[227] It is
usually assumed that the purpose of biblical language is to communicate information *about* what God has done and what God
wants the reader to do. But in addition to this extraverted function, biblical language also has an introverted, expressive function, which is critical for the emotional reaction to scripture
which we have been considering. If God is known, paradoxically, in "a cloud of unknowing," then it will be the expressive function of the Bible's language to point towards the ineffable mystery
and to dispose the reader to encounter it.

ORALITY AND AURALITY IN THE CHRISTIAN TRADITION

The importance of sound in reading the Bible is obvious
once we consider the primacy of the spoken word in Christian
tradition. "Gospel" meant oral proclamation, or *kerygma,*
before it came to designate a written text, and the word still
retains this older meaning today. Pliny refers to the use of
hymns in Christian worship,[228] and some of these hymns have
been preserved (e.g., Phil. 2:6–11). The Form Critics tell us that
the sayings of Jesus (prefaced by the introductory formula,
"Amen, amen, I *say* to you") went through a generation of oral
transmission before the first written Gospel was composed.
Christianity's attachment to the spoken word may have something to do with Jesus' relationship to the prophetic tradition, in
which divine revelation is prefaced with the introductory formula: "Thus *says* the Lord. . . ." Although all language is
ambiguous, spoken language, through personal contact and
contextualization, has a directness which is lacking in the end-
less "deferral" of writing. When Paul writes, "Scripture *says.* . .
." (Rom. 4:3), he is expressing a desire to retrieve the spoken
word of revelation through a text which, strictly speaking,
doesn't say anything.

---

227. Patrick Collins, *More Than Meets the Eye* (New York: Paulist
Press,1983), 68.
228. Epp. X, 96–97.

Christianity's first scripture was the Hebrew Bible (in Greek), but this scripture could only be of use for Christian faith if it was interpreted in a radically new way. Hence Paul's contrast between the "letter" of scripture and the "spirit" through which scripture acquires life-giving meaning for the Christian believer. The contrast between letter and spirit corresponds to the contrast between written and spoken language. Spoken language includes the breath (Latin *spiritus*), and the "spirit," like the wind (Greek *pneuma*), has the spontaneity and unpredictability of spoken language: "it blows where it will" (John 3:8).[229] Spontaneity and unpredictability are also characteristic of the "spiritual" reading of scripture, to which Paul appeals. The Christian church, which has felt free to reinterpret the Hebrew scriptures in accordance with its own faith, has privileged the oral performance of scripture.[230] Right down to the present day, scripture has always been read *aloud* during worship, and in this reading sound is obviously crucial. When scripture ceases to be memorized, recited, and experienced, its vitality in the life of the individual and the community tends to decrease.

Christianity began at a time when oral culture was only just giving way to written culture.[231] Writing was often an aid to oral performance, rather than an independent form of communication, and silent reading was virtually unknown.[232] Even today, when silent reading has become the norm, it is usually accompanied by involuntary vocalization.

---

229. See "Concerning the Word 'Spirit,'" Jung, *CW*, vol. 9, pt. 1, 208–14.

230. The two most significant studies on oral and written scriptures in world religions are: Harold Coward, *Sacred Word and Sacred Text* (Maryknoll, N.Y.: Orbis Books, 1988) and William Graham, *Beyond the Written Word* (Cambridge University Press, 1988).

231. Paul Achtemeier, "*Omne verbum sonat:* The New Testament and the Oral Environment of Late Western Antiquity," *Journal of Biblical Literature* 109 (1990), 3–27.

232. Ibid., 15–17. This was true even of solitary readers. St. Jerome complains in one of his letters that he is unable to read, because he has a sore throat!

THE ENGLISH REFORMATION AND THE "VERBAL ICON"

THERE IS A striking coincidence in the fact that the English Bible
was officially promulgated during the same reign which saw the
commencement of the attack on painted and sculpted images.[233]
According to Jung, the Protestant Reformation gave a major
impetus to the "intensification of rational consciousness"[234] that
now characterizes Western culture. Putting the biblical text in the
place formerly occupied by "the people's Bible"—i.e., statues,
images, and stained-glass windows—seems to signal a return to
what is both "the distinguishing mark of the Christian epoch" and
"the congenital vice of our age: the supremacy of the word."[235]
Does the dissemination of the vernacular Bible represent the triumph of conceptual thinking over imagistic thinking?

If we consider the matter more precisely, we see that the iconoclasm of the sixteenth century was not complete: in place of the
visual imagery of the medieval church, the English Reformation
substituted the "verbal icons" of the English Bible and *The Book
of Common Prayer*. If, as Jacques Lacan has suggested, "[t]he
unconscious is structured like a language,"[236] then we can understand why the sound of the English Bible has played such an
important role in our religious history. Northrop Frye quotes
from the King James Bible in his book *The Great Code*, but (as
mentioned earlier) in explaining why he has chosen to do this,
he explicitly excludes considerations of sound: "I use it [the
KJV] not because of the beauty of its cadences: conventional
aesthetic canons of that sort I wanted to get rid of at the start."[237]
In this extraordinary statement Frye devalues an aspect of scripture which is of critical importance in all religious traditions
which have a scripture.

---

233. Cf. Eamon Duffy, *The Stripping of the Altars* (New Haven: Yale
University Press, 1992).

234. Jung, *CW*, vol. 11, 199.

235. Ibid., vol. 10, 286.

236. Jacques Lacan, *The Language of the Self*, trans. Anthony Wilden
(Baltimore: Johns Hopkins Press, 1968), 32.

237. Frye, *The Great Code*, xiii.

Is Language Symbolic?

SUCH DEVALUATION OF phonetic considerations can be traced to the position of de Saussure, who claimed that the relationship between the signifier and the signified (or the object of reference?) was purely arbitrary. This view weighs heavily against regarding the linguistic sign as a symbol, since a symbol implies "a natural bond between the signifier and the signified."[238]

Paul Kugler has shown that while the relation between sound and meaning may not be symbolic, the relationship *between signs* is another matter. In *The Interpretation of Dreams,* Freud had already noted how a particular dream made use of the similarity between the words "violet" and "violate" in order to express "in the language of flowers" the dreamer's thoughts on the "violence" of defloration. Freud called this an instance of the "verbal bridges" crossed by the paths leading to the unconscious.[239] The unconscious tends to construct images according to phonetic considerations.[240]

But unlike Freud, who considered this similarity in phonetic patterns to be chance or arbitrary, Kugler has shown that the phonetic pattern of significantly related words reveals an invariance which transcends language differences. The quality of an individual sound may have no symbolic significance, but the invariant relationship *between* sounds points to an archetypal dimension of language. The linguistic complex is a system of manifold cross-references, in which the individual word represents but one element in a web of associations; a single word can never be properly understood in itself. At the unconscious level, the quality of these associations shifts from the semantic

238. Quoted in Kugler, *Alchemy of Discourse,* 51.

239. Sigmund Freud, *Interpretation of Dreams,* trans. James Strachey (New York: Avon Books, 1972), 410.

240. Cf. the lines from Gerard Manley Hopkins's poem "Hurrahing in Harvest:"

> *And the azurous hung hills are his world-wielding shoulder*
> *Majestic—as a stallion stalwart, very-violet-sweet!—*

to the phonetic.[241] Consequently, the communicative function of language, i.e., its ability to communicate ideas, is not its only function. The phonetic links which bind together the linguistic system of the unconscious enable language to "speak" directly to the soul.

THE PROBLEM OF BIBLE TRANSLATION

SINCE CHRISTIANITY HAS never separated the semantic and phonetic dimensions of religious language, the phonetic dimension of the Bible can only function in a vernacular translation which is "understanded of the people." This need not mean the everyday vernacular which is *spoken* by the people. Biblical English does not have to be colloquial, but it must be capable of being remembered and loved by those who hear it used.

It is unfortunate, from the perspective of biblical empirics, that literary and phonetic considerations have been assigned such a low priority in the updating of religious language. T. S. Eliot, an uncooperative recruit in the 1950s to the commission for the updating of the Psalter, was outspoken in his rejection of the New English Bible (1961), finding in its translations "something which astonishes in its combination of the vulgar, the trivial and the pedantic; we ask in alarm: 'What is happening to the English language?'"[242] Contrast the statement of the eminent New Testament scholar, Dennis Nineham, about biblical translations used in worship:

---

241. Consider the following verbal structures (Kugler, *Alchemy of Discourse,* 52):

flower	deflower	defloration
carnation	carnal	carnage
violet	violate	violent

In each verbal structure representing a transformation of the "flower" complex an invariant phonetic pattern moves from "flo" to "carn" to "viol." Kugler shows the same invariant pattern in German and Hungarian.

242. "T. S. Eliot on the Language of the New English Bible," *The Sunday Telegraph* 16 (December 1962), 7.

[People] did not go to church primarily for an aesthetic fillip; but to worship God and to hear the Word mediated to them through the Bible; and therefore, surely the first question was whether that was as good an instrument as they could find for purveying the meaning of God's Word and allowing that Word to have its maximum impact.

That was the question which should be uppermost in their minds and not questions about whether the New English Bible was as beautiful or as dignified as it could be.[243]

What people respond to in biblical translations is doubtless as varied as the translations themselves. Many expect to find what is chiefly valued by the prevailing culture: historical accuracy, clarity, intelligibility, and, in most recent years, political correctness. But it must be said that these values, important as they may be, do not necessarily correspond to the laws of the psyche. True religious language, Evelyn Underhill observes,

enchants and informs, addressing its rhythmic and symbolic speech to regions of the mind which are inaccessible to argument, and evoking moments of awe and love which no exhortation can obtain. It has meaning at many levels, and welds together all those who use it; overriding their personal moods, and subduing them to its grave loveliness.[244]

If there are those who feel moved by the Authorized Version, despite its inadequate scholarship and insensitivity to modern cultural concerns, this is a reaction which biblical empirics must take seriously and not dismiss as sentimental obscurantism. Undoubtedly, familiarity has something to do with it, but the emotional response may also reflect an appreciation of the cadences and aural appeal which Frye chose to ignore. For whatever its other limitations, the Authorized Version came into being during the greatest period in the literary history of England, when language was much more than simply the vehicle for communication.

---

243. Quoted in R. C. D. Jasper, *The Development of the Anglican Liturgy 1662–1980* (SPCK, 1989), 295.

244. Evelyn Underhill, *Worship* (London: Nisbet, 1937), 113.

THE LANGUAGE OF THE HEART

The function of religious language is to embody what it is like, in the phrase of T. S. Eliot, to *"feel* towards God."[245] There is a clarity of statement which suits material objects but which simply does not apply to spiritual things. For biblical language to function expressively, aesthetic and especially phonetic considerations are crucial, and not a mere "fillip," as Nineham would have it. Words put the reader in a spiritual state of mind and sensibility as much by their cadence and aural appeal as by their precise meaning. In the words of the late Marshall McLuhan, "The medium is the message." The Indian tradition distinguishes words with power, or mantras, from ordinary words.[246] Perhaps this may provide an explanation for the experience of those who claim to be able to hear the divine through some biblical translations, but not through others.

In recent studies of newborns, it has emerged that parents

> appear to help babies learn by adopting the rhythmic, high-pitched speaking style known as Parentese. When speaking to babies, Stanford University psychologist Anne Fernald has found, mothers and fathers from many cultures change their speech patterns in the same peculiar ways. "They put their faces very close to the child," she reports. "They use shorter utterances, and *they speak in an unusually melodious fashion." The heart rate of infants increases while listening to Parentese,* even Parentese delivered in a foreign language [emphases mine]. [247]

Charles Darwin is said to have believed that the power of producing and appreciating music existed before the power of speech was arrived at. If this is so, then the experience of present-day infants parallels the evolution of the human race, insofar as the musical intonations of "baby talk" precede and facilitate the acquisition of language: ontogeny imitates phylogeny. The

---

245. T. S. Eliot, "The Social Function of Poetry" in *On Poetry and Poets* (London: Faber and Faber, 1957), 25.

246. Coward and Goa, *Mantra,* 43.

247. J. Madeleine Nash, "How a Child's Brain Develops," *Time,* June 9, 1997, 46–54.

reaction of babies' hearts to "the exaggerated, vowel-rich sounds of Parentese" gives new significance to Hos. 2:14, where God declares that he "will speak to the heart" of Israel, as he seeks to woo her back to a faithful covenant relationship.

In expressive language, conceptuality is not abolished but transcended, by engaging an underlying deep structure which imaginally connects disparate concepts. Behind and beneath the word there is always something more ultimate: the image, which is the expression of archetypal energy that is simply there. As Jung has written,

> The protean mythologem and the shimmering symbol express the processes of the psyche far more trenchantly and, in the end, far more clearly than the clearest concept; for the symbol not only conveys a visualization of the process but—and this is per-haps just as important—it also brings a re-experiencing of it.[248]

---

248. Jung, *CW*, vol. 13, 162–63.

5. The Key of Knowledge

That which you have will save you if you
bring it forth from yourselves.
—The Gospel of Thomas

The Nag Hammadi Library

UNLIKE THE DEAD Sea Scrolls, which were also discovered around 1945 but which cast no direct light on Christian origins, the Nag Hammadi library contains an interpretation of Christianity whose existence has always been known, but whose literature had been largely suppressed. One of the characteristics of these texts is an emphasis on "knowledge," Greek *gnosis*, the word by which this interpretation of Christianity has come to be known. What is meant specifically by this term is a religious knowledge which is experiential and transformative and originates from within. These characteristics emerge in the first saying of the best known of the Nag Hammadi texts, *The Gospel of Thomas*, "Whoever finds the interpretation of these sayings will not taste death."

Where Did Gnosis Come From?

THE STRIKING DIFFERENCES between this literature and other early Christian writings has led some to conclude that it represents a late distortion of the Christian gospel, brought about by pagan syncretism.[249] However, Rudolf Bultmann and his followers have seen

---

249. E. M. Yamauchi, "Gnosticism and Early Christianity" in *Hellenization Revisited*, ed. W. E. Helleman (Lanham, Md.: University Press of America, 1994), 29–67.

the origins of Christian gnosis in the New Testament itself.[250] This view is confirmed by early church writers who attribute the beginnings of gnosis to Simon Magus, a Samaritan convert of Philip (Acts 8:13), whose followers declared him to be "that power of God which is called Great" (Acts 8:10).[251] Gnosis would therefore seem to be a development within Christianity and not a pagan import.

Within the New Testament canon, Paul and the author of the Fourth Gospel, not to mention Jesus himself, exhibit a spiritual knowledge which commended them to later Gnostic writers. But Paul's letters and the Johannine corpus also show a concern for the threat that religious individualism can represent for any collective church structure.

GNOSIS VS. "SOUND DOCTRINE"

THE CREATIVE TENSION which we find in these New Testament writings was abandoned in later letters attributed to Paul, where "what is falsely called knowledge" (1 Tim. 6:20), with its "myths and genealogies," was rejected in favor of "sound doctrine" (1 Tim. 1:4,10; 4:7; 6:3; 2 Tim. 1:13; 4:3,4; Titus 1:9,14; 2:1; 3:9). "The word of faith" (Rom. 10:8), which comes from hearing the preacher (Rom. 10:14), is thus opposed to the imaginative and mythic forms of introverted religious knowledge.

The culmination of this "logocentric" emphasis is found in the words of Irenaeus:

> True knowledge is that which consists in the doctrine of the apostles, and the ancient constitution of the church throughout all the world, and the distinctive manifestation of the body of Christ according to the successions of the bishops, by which

---

250. Kurt Rudolph, *Gnosis* (San Francisco: Harper & Row, 1987), 32–33. I have deliberately avoided the neologism "Gnosticism." See G. J. M. Robinson, "On Bridging the Gulf From Q to the Gospel of Thomas (or Vice Versa)," *Nag Hammadi, Gnosticism, and Early Christianity*, C. W. Hedrick and Robert Hodgson, Jr., eds. (Peabody, Mass.: Hendrickson Publishers, 1986), especially the section, "The Messina Definition of Gnosticism, " 128–35.

251. Gerd Lüdemann, *Untersuchungen zur simonianischen Gnosis* (Göttingen: Vandenhoeck & Ruprecht, 1975).

they have handed down that church which exists in every place (*AH* IV.33.8).

For the Gnostics, those who make such claims "speak of things which they do not understand" and "boast that the mystery of truth is theirs alone" (*Apocalypse of Peter* 76:29–30). "Those people are dry canals" (79:30).

PRIMARY AND SECONDARY RELIGION

HERE WE SEE two different understandings of revelation, corresponding to the distinction made by William James: "Churches, when once established, live at second-hand upon tradition; but the *founders* of every church owed their power originally to the fact of their direct personal communion with the divine."[252]

Paul writes of his purpose in life in the following terms: "that I may know Christ and the power of his resurrection" (Phil. 3:10). To "know" the power of Christ's resurrection is a curious expression, and the New English Bible substitutes the word "experience" in the second half of the clause. This underlines the fact that the knowledge in question is not the objective, communicable knowledge that comes from without but the transformative, experiential knowledge that comes from within.

However, when Paul assumed his missionary role, he made use of kerygmatic formulations which, though derived from his own faith experience, were now used to communicate "the faith" to the prospective convert, who is summoned to accept them in obedience (Rom. 1:5). There thus arises a fundamental distinction between Paul the "founder," whose conversion to Christ was the result of a personal religious experience, and those whose conversion consisted in becoming "obedient to the standard of teaching" (Rom. 6:17) proposed by the missionary, and in living "at second hand" upon this tradition.

But not all Christians were content with this. Although one group accepts Paul's claim that seeing the Lord is a privilege restricted to the apostles ("*Last of all,* [Christ] appeared also to

---

252. James, *Varieties of Religious Experience,* 49.

me" [1 Cor. 15:8]), and bases its faith upon the apostolic witness, the other group claims continuing access to the same sort of experience which Paul had enjoyed. For such Christians it is the immediacy and power of personal experience that determines the truth of a belief, not the other way around.

Jung's View of Gnosis

C. G. Jung recognized the psychological dimension of Gnostic writings, which gives them significance for contemporary religious thought. No longer can they be dismissed as a curious relic from late antiquity. However, the first major publication of a Nag Hammadi text, *The Gospel of Thomas*, did not take place until 1959, just two years before Jung's death. His knowledge of Christian gnosis was therefore based on very limited source material. Nevertheless, he saw in the Gnostic writings the characteristic which makes them so important for our study: to an extent unparalleled in canonical scripture, the Gnostics allowed themselves to be influenced by inner experience. They are, therefore, "a veritable mine of information concerning all those natural symbols arising out of the repercussion of the Christian message."[253] Although Jung was not referring specifically to the Gnostic reading of scripture, his words have an obvious significance for this question.

While some Nag Hammadi texts may have been used in catachesis and rites of initiation, their bizarre exegesis of scripture seems to have resulted from the same sort of reading as Jung's reading of the Book of Job. June Singer has written: "Gnosis is based not in the understanding of the mind but in the sensibility of the heart."[254]

> Their [the Gnostics'] "history" as they committed it to writing is a true mythology, having no relation to external happenings but representing their inner experiences of vision, fantasy, or imagination projected onto both the visible, material world and the invisible, spiritual world to which they claimed a special access.[255]

---

253. Jung, *CW*, vol. 9, pt. 2, 269.
254. June Singer, *A Gnostic Book of Hours* (San Francisco: Harper SanFrancisco, 1992), xix.
255. Ibid., 149.

The impact of scripture upon the heart is precisely what we have been calling "biblical empirics," and a reading of scripture that is governed by "the sensibility of the heart" may provide an ancient example of the phenomenon which we have been discussing.

THE GNOSTIC PROTEST AGAINST THE COSMOS

THE GNOSTIC EXPERIENCE of scripture cannot be separated from the Gnostic experience of the world, for gnosis "brings us face to face with one of the more radical answers of man to his predicament and with the insights which only that radical position could bring forth. . . ."[256]

According to Walter Wink, "The blemish which [the Gnostics] saw in nature lay not in its chaos . . . , but in an excess of order,"[257] which had resulted from the collapse of the city states and the dominance of the Roman Empire. The distinction between nature and society, which modern thinking takes for granted, was far less obvious in antiquity. The Gnostics' experience of society's oppressive structures led them to attribute creation not to a good God but to an ignorant demiurge. This is the origin of the dualism between the fallen cosmos and the divine *pleroma,* to which the Gnostic seeks to escape.

ANTHROPOLOGICAL DUALISM

TO THIS COSMOLOGICAL dualism is added the anthropological dualism between body (or flesh) and spirit, which is also found in Paul (especially Gal. 5:17). The fantasy of a separation of the soul from the body (cf. Phil. 1:23) represents the culmination of an initial psychic ascetic stage, which for Jung means a freedom from the constrictive powers of instinctual and destabilizing emotionality.[258] But whereas Jung's psychology moves from this ascetic stage back

---

256. Hans Jonas, *The Gnostic Religion,* 2d ed. (Boston: Beacon Press, 1963), xvii.

257. Walter Wink, *Cracking the Gnostic Code* (Atlanta, Ga.: Scholars Press, 1993), 2. The original meaning of the Greek word *kosmos* is "order."

258. Jung, *CW,* vol. 14, 471.

into embodiment, the Gnostic seeks to pass through "the window into eternity"[259] and away from the confines of finitude.

The Gnostics' negative attitudes toward the body, sexuality, and the whole material world were widely shared in late antiquity and were not a specifically Gnostic phenomenon. In blaming the body for the soul's forgetfulness and in making it the scapegoat for human ignorance, the Gnostics were simply projecting onto the body *their own* ignorance of the body itself. The darkly pessimistic Gnostic world view should not lead us to dismiss an approach to Christian symbolism which has profound psychological significance,[260] as well as the potential to renew the faltering structures of Western religion. Christian gnosis is "one of the great moments of the recovery of the power of myth in the ancient world."[261]

EPISTEMOLOGICAL DUALISM

SINCE WHATEVER IS unknown to consciousness can only be known through projection, psychological contents in a pre-psychological age can only find expression in what is perceived to be external, e.g., the physical body, the cosmic drama of creation and redemption, or the apocalyptic scenario. Such projections are more evident in the palpable mythology of Gnostic literature than in our canonical books.

Underlying both the cosmic and the anthropological dualism is the fundamental opposition between ignorance and truth, which is available only through gnosis. Gnostic dualism must be seen in relation to the monistic belief in the unity from which all things have come and to which they must ultimately return.[262] The

---

259. Ibid., 473.

260. Irenaeus himself seems to have recognized the psychological thrust of his opponents' writings: "they speak of what is 'without' and what 'within' in reference to knowledge and ignorance and not with respect to local distance" (AH II.4.2).

261. Peter Brown, *The Body and Society* (New York: Columbia University Press), 107.

262. Cf. Rudolph, *Gnosis,* 86. A fourteenth-century alchemical manuscript represents the universe as a serpent biting its tail, with the Greek inscription "One is the All" (Ibid., 70).

unity which is at the root of the cosmos cannot be grasped by the ordering strategies of rational consciousness.

The Gnostics despised the body as a symbol of ignorance and forgetfulness. The coming of the soul into matter makes it forget its heavenly origin and become involved in worldly cares. The role of gnosis is to provide a wake-up call which reminds the soul of its origin and destiny, so that it awakes from the nightmare of worldly existence. (*The Gospel of Truth* 29:10)

This motif of remembrance[263] finds expression in "The Hymn of the Pearl," from *The Acts of Thomas*. The king's son, upon arriving in Egypt, falls into forgetfulness and receives a letter from home with the summons:"Remember that though you are the son of kings, you have fallen under a servile yoke" (110:44). The Gnostic yearning to return from the multiplicity of creation to the primordial unity of being has distinctly mystical implications.

GNOSTIC EXEGESIS OF SCRIPTURE

THE GNOSTIC PROTEST against "the powers that be" is paralleled in the Gnostics' reading of sacred scripture. The Gnostics and the orthodox had the same scripture, but they read it differently. The directed thinking which is characteristic of doctrinal orthodoxy leads to directed reading: the reader constructs a story "behind" the text. A directed reading of the opening chapters of Genesis leads to the orderly sequence of "salvation history" which is familiar to us from dogmatic theology: the creation of the world, the creation of Adam and Eve, the Fall, and the promise of redemption (Gen. 3:15). In such an "objective" reading, a distinction must be made between the "historical" events (objective redemption) and the appropriation of this redemption by the individual (subjective redemption).

The Gnostics' disregard for the wording and traditional interpretation of scripture has led Kurt Rudolph to speak of a "protest exegesis."[264] In his study, "The Breaking of Form," the literary critic Harold Bloom speaks of the reading encounter as a combat,

---

263. The psychological significance of remembrance finds expression in Freud's injunction: "Stop repeating and start remembering!"

264. Rudolph, *Gnosis,* 54.

out of which meaning is wrested. Reading springs from the will to clear space for the reader over against a menacingly strong text, and it is therefore not a polite process. Bloom mentions the Gnostic exegesis of scripture as "a salutary act of textual violence, transgressive through-and-through."[265]

The ceaseless crisscrossing and interweaving of themes and characters preclude referentiality: the feminine characters in particular—Barbelo, Sophia, the serpent, heavenly Eve, Epinoia—all seem to be expressions of the same force, rather like Olympia, Antonia, and Giulietta in Offenbach's opera *Tales of Hoffmann*. The Gnostic creation stories do not show us a world distinct from ourselves: "objective" reality is renounced for the sake of an imaginal noesis which can exist only in a twilight which rational clarity dispels.[266]

Gnostic interpretation of scripture gives free reign to the inner promptings of the imagination. The text serves as a catalyst for the release of natural symbols arising out of the unconscious, and the text becomes, in turn, the screen upon which these unconscious contents are projected. The inner is expressed in terms of the outer. By pointing away from itself, in order to express an experience which is beyond rational discourse, the imagistic language of gnosis forestalls any idolatry of the word. Gnostic writing does not point to self-consistent and unchanging realities beyond the empirical world but rather uses religious images to interpret existence.[267] This strategy of "resistant reading," which is also used today in feminist literary criticism, is "a self-defensive measure designed to clear imaginative space beyond the influential web of the traditional script."[268]

INDICATIONS OF NONCONCEPTUAL PROCESSES IN GNOSTIC EXEGESIS

BUT WHAT EVIDENCE is there that the Gnostic reading of scripture is the symbolic expression of "the repercussion of the Christian

265. Harold Bloom, *Deconstruction and Criticism* (New York: Seabury Press, 1979), 6.

266. Jung, *CW,* vol. 13, 163.

267. Michael LaFargue, *Language and Gnosis* (Philadelphia: Fortress, 1985), 207.

268. Willi Braun, "Resisting John," *Studies in Religion* 19 (1990), 64.

message" on the "inner experience" of the reader, and not an artificial superimposition upon the text of extraneous material, like Paul's superimposition of the doctrine of justification by faith upon the Hagar story?

There is a passage from *The Gospel of Truth* which suggests the importance that nonconceptual processes seem to have had in Gnostic exegesis:

> For it is not the ears that smell the fragrance, but (it is) the breath that has the sense of smell and attracts the fragrance to itself and is submerged in the fragrance of the Father. . . .[269]

In the orthodox conception, hearing is the most important sense, since it is through hearing that the word of faith is received (Rom. 10:8.14.17). The Gnostic, however, is the "fragrance" of the Father, and what comes through the ears is less effective, less direct, and less intimate than what comes through *pneuma,* which has the double meaning of "spirit" and "breath."

The Gospel of Truth is an instructive example of the way scripture is used in Valentinian gnosis:

> Valentinus never quotes or cites a text in GTr but rather incorporates allusions so that no seams are visible; in other words, his interpretations are interwoven with his allusions.[270]

This absence of explicit scriptural citation inhibits any distinction between text and interpretation. The reader has no possibility of reconstructing some reality *behind* the text: what the reader reads is what the reader gets. Nor can the reader distinguish between "then" and "now." "Salvation history" is inseparable from the psychic awakening of the reader.

THE USE OF SCRIPTURE IN *THE GOSPEL OF TRUTH*

AT THE EXACT center of *The Gospel of Truth* we find the beatitude: "Blessed is the one who has opened the eyes of the blind" (30:14–16). In the canonical Gospels there are stories which

---

269. *The Gospel of Truth* 34:9–14.
270. J. A. Williams, *Biblical Interpretation in the Gnostic Gospel of Truth from Nag Hammadi* (Atlanta, Ga.: Scholars Press, 1988), 11.

narrate the healing of blind persons, the most notable being the dramatic Johannine account of the healing of the man born blind.[271] However, nothing in *The Gospel of Truth* requires a reference to such a miracle of Jesus, to say nothing of *limiting* the beatitude to such a reference. "The one who opens the eyes of the blind" could equally well be a Gnostic teacher. It could be the serpent in the Genesis story, who is sometimes a benevolent character in Gnostic exegesis, since it is through the serpent's intervention that the eyes of Adam and Eve are opened (3:7). Or it could be Sophia, who rouses the divine sparks from the forgetful slumber of existence in the cosmos.

Any and all of these possible references can be understood symbolically in terms of the process of psychic awakening in the reader. Not only does the art of the Gnostic evangelist abolish the distinction between "then" and "now," between objective and subjective redemption. It equally abolishes the distinction between the different *segments* of salvation history: the creation of the cosmos and the creation of Adam and Eve; creation, redemption, and eschatological fulfilment.[272]

In Gnostic exegesis, to use the words of the pre-Socratic philosopher Anaxagoras, "everything is in everything else."[273] The reader is free to relate his or her own inner world to the imaginal world of the beatitude and to adopt any "horizon" that he or she prefers, without any need to project it onto "the intention of the author."

Following the beatitude is a passage which also might suggest one of Jesus' healing miracles: "Having extended his hand to him who lay upon the ground, he set him up on his feet" (30:19–22).[274] However, the subject of this sentence is not "Jesus" but "the spirit" (30:17), and the sentence continues "for

---

271. John 9; cf. 11:37; also Matt 11:5; Luke 7:21–22; Mark 8:22–26; Matt 9:27–31; Mark 10:46–52 and parallels.

272. Rudolph, *Gnosis,* 95: "These two sections of this 'primal history' [i.e., cosmogony and anthropogony] belong closely together and are only artificially separated by us."

273. Hermann Diels, *Die Fragmente der Vorsokratiker* (Berlin: Weidmannsche Verlagsbuchhandlung, 1952), vol.2, 32 (my translation).

274. Cf. Mark 2:1–12 and parallels; John 5:1–18.

he had not yet risen" (30:22–23). Although an allusion to the descent of the spirit on Christ at his crucifixion has been suggested, as well as a reference to the resurrection, the passage does not directly allude to Christ at all. The imagery used here "ultimately derives from traditional Jewish speculation about the primal man, who lay inert upon the earth, before being vivified by the insufflation of the divine breath."[275]

One might think of Michelangelo's famous representation of the creation of Adam in the Sistine Chapel, in which God extends his life-giving hand to touch the inert hand of Adam, who is lying on the ground. Whatever specific reference is preferred, the image suggests the "new creation" of the human being who receives the revelatory gnosis.

A little further on, we read a version of the parable of the lost sheep,[276] followed by the words, "Even on the sabbath, he labored for the sheep which he found fallen into the pit" (32:18–20).[277] The indefinite reference of the pronoun dehistoricizes the allusions to the canonical Gospels. No longer are they limited to Jesus' justification for his scandalous practices of associating with sinners and healing on the sabbath. The historical specificity of the canonical parallels is undermined, and they return to the imaginal world from which they came.

In *The Gospel of Truth* the parables of Jesus can be extended to include the Father's search for the All, which is from the Father, yet ignorant of the Father. Through conversion from ignorance to gnosis, the individual participates in the cosmic drama of the return of the All to its root in the Godhead.[278]

In all these examples the images in the canonical texts are freed from the constraints of doctrinal or historical interpretation, so that they become able to generate that experience of expanded consciousness which, in the Christian tradition, goes by the name of "revelation." For the Gnostic, as for Kierkegaard ("Truth is

---

275. *Nag Hammadi Codex I (The Jung Codex)* NHS 22–23 (Leiden: Brill, 1985), 86.

276. Cf. Matt 18:12–14 and parallel.

277. Cf. John 5:17; Luke 14:5.

278. Cf. Anne McGuire, "Conversion and Gnosis in the *Gospel of Truth,*" *Novum Testamentum* 28:4 (1986), 338–55.

THE KEY OF KNOWLEDGE / *125*

subjectivity"), religious truth is connected with the subject rather than with the object.

GNOSTIC "INCONSISTENCY"

CONCEPTUAL THINKING IS essential for the formation, preservation, and transmission of a stable body of doctrine. The Gnostics, however, had no normative theology,[279] and, with their frankly mythological interpretation of the Christian symbol system, were under no obligation to avoid self-contradiction. Irenaeus writes:

> Let us now look at the inconsistent opinions of those heretics (for there are some two or three of them), how they do not agree in treating the same points, but alike, in things and names, set forth opinions mutually discordant (*AH* I,xi,1).

Gnostic "inconsistency," like the many-headed hydra of Greek legend (*AH* I,xxx,15), is a reflection of the imagistic basis of Gnostic exegesis, where the principle of contradiction has no application: "This creative urge explains the bewildering confusion, the kaleidoscopic changes and syncretistic regroupings, the continual rejuvenation of myths in Greek culture."[280]

THE GNOSTIC USE OF LANGUAGE

INSTEAD OF USING language to try to construct a rationally consistent theological system, the Gnostics related the word to the image through which the divine is revealed. In *Thunder, Perfect Mind,* Sophia proclaims, "I am . . . the word whose appearance is multiple."[281] *The Gospel of Philip* declares, "Truth did not come into the world naked, but it came in types and images. The world will not receive truth in any other way."[282]

---

279. Rudolph, *Gnosis,* 53.
280. Jung, *CW,* vol. 5, 20–21.
281. *The Thunder, Perfect Mind* 14:14.
282. *The Gospel of Philip* 67:9–10.

Using the paired opposites which are characteristic of mythic speech, Sophia declares,

> *I am the honored and the scorned one.*
> *I am the whore and the holy one.*
> *I am the wife and the virgin.*
> *I am the mother and the daughter.*[283]

The primacy of the image in Gnostic writing and the lack of concern for rational consistency suggest that we are dealing here with poetic discourse and not with a doctrinal system. Behind and beneath the word there is always something more ultimate: the image, which is the expression of an archetypal energy which is simply there. Archetypal interpretation, as a form of resistant reading, is more congenial to the poetics of the lyric, which allows a role for intuition and subjectivity. It is interesting to note that a connection has been made between the Cathars, who continued the Gnostic tradition during the Middle Ages, and the troubadours.[284]

GNOSTIC USE OF DECONSTRUCTION

THE DOCTRINAL INTERPRETATION (and discreditation) of gnosis ignores not only the central importance given to the image but also some clearly deconstructionist statements about language. The *Trimorphic Protennoia* implies an "excavation of language" in the statement, "I had gone down below their [the Archons'] language." (41:26–27) Particularly in *The Gospel of Philip* the author wrestles with the paradox that language, though brought into the world by truth, is nevertheless the cause of error.

In an extraordinary anticipation of Jacques Derrida, we find this statement about the differential nature of language: "Light and darkness, life and death, right and left, are brothers of one another. They are inseparable."[285] From this it follows that nothing can be

---

283. *The Thunder, Perfect Mind* 13:19–20.

284. de Rougemont, 75–82: "Courtly Love: Troubadours and Cathars."

285. *The Gospel of Philip* 53:14–16.

understood in isolation: "Because of this neither are the good good, nor the evil evil, nor is life life, nor death death."[286]

The text goes on to draw the consequences for "God talk":

> Thus one who hears the word "God" does not perceive what is correct, but perceives what is incorrect. So also with "the father" and "the son" and "the holy spirit" and "life" and "light" and "resurrection" and "the church" and all the rest.[287]

The literalistic interpretation of religious language leads to deception, which only the inner knowledge of the Gnostic can escape. These explicit statements give us an indication of what kind of language game is being played.[288]

A GNOSTIC PARABLE ABOUT LANGUAGE

THERE IS AN obscure passage in *The Gospel of Philip* which suggests the contrast between the rational and the archetypal dimensions of language. The text stresses the difference between creating and begetting: a creator works openly, but begetting is done in private.[289]

In the Gnostic creation myth it is the demiurge and his archons who create Adam from the elements. But Adam has no real life in him. Only the highest being can confer upon him the divinity that will exalt him above the demiurge and make him capable of receiving salvation.[290] The demiurge who vainly boasts, "I am a jealous God [Exod 20:5]; besides me there is no god [Isa 45:5]," corresponds psychologically to the rational ego, which proclaims its self-sufficiency, unaware of its own roots in the unconscious.

The primary expression of ego consciousness is rational discourse. It "works openly," i.e., it is exoteric, and it relies for its intelligibility upon social convention. Begetting is an esoteric

---

286. Ibid. 53:17–19.
287. Ibid. 53:27–32.
288. Kurt Rudolph, "Philosophy of Names" in *Images of the Feminine in Gnosticism,* ed. Karen King (Philadelphia: Fortress, 1988), 230–32.
289. *The Gospel of Philip* 81:14–82:2.
290. Rudolph, *Gnosis,* 94–95.

action, done "in private," away from ego consciousness. It is also instinctual, thus paralleling the archetypes, which, like biological instincts, "direct all fantasy activity into its appointed paths."[291]

If understood with reference to language, "begetting" can refer to the unconscious associations which are grouped around an archetypal image. The author challenges the orthodox view that the same creator God is responsible for both the creation of the world and the begetting of the Son: "he who creates cannot beget." That is to say, rational discourse and fantasy language come from different parts of the psyche. Gnostic texts are esoteric because their meaning depends not on public conventions of rational discourse but on correspondences hidden in the deep structure of language, to which ego consciousness has no direct access.

"BEGOTTEN, NOT CREATED"

ACCORDING TO THE instruction of Father Zosima in Dostoevsky's novel *The Brothers Karamazov*,

> Much on earth is hidden from us, but to make up for that we have been given a precious mystic sense of our living bond with the other world, with the higher heavenly world, and the roots of our thoughts and feelings are not here but in other worlds.[292]

For the Gnostic, the link between "things visible and invisible" is founded not on an act of creation but on a begetting from above (cf. John 3:3). The connection between the visible image and its invisible source is the result of inner process, like the resemblance between a woman's child and the man who loves her.[293]

Consequently, the paradigm for the Gnostic use of language is to be sought not in the Word's creative power but in the eternal process of generation through which the Word came to be: "begotten, not created." The hidden correspondences between the two

---

291. Jung, *CW,* vol. 9, pt. 1, 66.
292. Trans. Constance Barnett (New York: Norton, 1976), 299. Cf. Rudolph, *Gnosis,* 88: "the deep and hidden relation to this higher world."
293. *The Gospel of Philip* 78:12–13.

worlds are expressed not through rational discourse, the creation of ego consciousness, but through the power of fantasy language, which wells up from the deep structure which is eternally there.

ANDROGYNY AND THE FEMININE IN GNOSTICISM

ONE OF THE striking characteristics of Gnostic literature is the centrality of female figures. Sophia, whose place in canonical scripture is limited to a few powerful passages, is a central actor in the Gnostic redemption myth, and we encounter other female characters not found at all in the canonical writings: Norea, Edem, and Epinoia. The serpent too is construed as feminine. This phenomenon naturally attracts attention at the present time, when feminist hermeneutics has taken its rightful place in biblical exegesis.

However, it seems unlikely that this characteristic of the Gnostic writings is the result of some protofeminist agenda. We know too little about the actual status of women in Gnostic communities to be able to say that their situation was essentially different from that of women in other social contexts in the Greco–Roman world. The extended use of feminine imagery seems rather to be a natural correction, originating in the psyche, of the one-sidedly masculine symbolism of the canonical texts, which has been attributed to patriarchal influence. The feminine, which had been pushed to the margin, returns to a central position, and the integrity of the symbol, as a union of opposites, is restored.

The use of both masculine and feminine imagery leads naturally to androgyny as a central symbol in Gnostic mythology. Scholars of gnosis often interpret androgyny as though it were the replacement of sexuality through an asexual neuter. Those who read these texts from a Jungian perspective see androgyny rather as a symbolic representation of psychic complementarity, including the masculine and feminine aspects which are present in every individual personality, regardless of biological gender.

SEXUALITY

GNOSTICS AND ORTHODOX seem to be guided by two different root metaphors, both of them derived from a common scripture. In the Genesis story, creation comes about through God's word:

"God said . . ., and it was so." The prologue to the Fourth Gospel personifies this divine word: "The Word was with God . . ., and without him not one thing came into being" (John 1:1, 3). The masculine Logos replaces the feminine figure of Sophia, who, according to the Old Testament wisdom tradition, was beside God "like a master worker" (Prov. 8:30).

In the Gnostic creation story Sophia becomes the protagonist. She is given the epithet *prouneikos,*[294] which suggests impetuosity, wantonness, libido, in the inclusive sense used by Jung of any form of psychic energy.[295] As the connecting principle between the Deity and creation, Sophia, on the one hand, is God's "delight," while, on the other hand, she is "delighting in the human race" (Prov. 8:30–31).

In the Johannine prologue, where the feminine principle has been excluded, the sexual imagery is still implicit, insofar as the incarnate Word is the "Father's only Son" (John 1:14). But in the Gnostic reading, sexuality is not merely implied. Rather, it replaces speech as the root metaphor.[296] The beginning of the cosmic process is not the divine word but an act of autoeroticism. Sophia conceives a thought from herself, through the invisible spirit's foreknowledge, and reveals an image from herself, but without her consort's approval.[297]

The importance of sexual imagery in Gnostic literature is another indication of psychological factors at work in the Gnostic reading of scripture. For, on the one hand, sex is "the human function *par excellence,* that which determines indeed the incessant cycles of birth and death."[298] On the other hand, "man's sexuality" is one

---

294. Anne Pasquier, "Prouneikos" in *Images of the Feminine,* 47–66.

295. Jung, *CW,* vol. 5, 132–70.

296. Rudolph, *Gnosis,* 110 refers to the "erotic and sexual tenor" of *The Exegesis on the Soul* as "[a] striking feature," adding that this "is often found in gnostic texts in the description of life in this world."

297. *Apocryphon of John* 9:25–10:5.

298. Mircea Eliade, *Techniques du Yoga,* 199, quoted in de Rougemont, *Love in the Western World,* 116.

of "those facets of humanity which he finds most difficult to reconcile with his rational nature."[299]

In the New Testament the celibate state is placed above marriage (Matt. 19:12; 1 Cor. 7:8, 38), but the Gnostics went still further, rejecting marriage altogether. It is therefore striking, though scarcely surprising from a psychological viewpoint, that what was consciously excluded on the behavioral level appears as the central symbol of the Gnostic myth. In the Adam and Eve story, death comes into being through the separation of Eve from Adam, and it will only be overcome through the reintegration of the masculine with the feminine, as symbolized by the sexual act.[300]

This reintegration takes place in the sacrament of the bridal chamber, through which the soul (conceived of as feminine) is reunited with her angelic counterpart (conceived of as masculine). This sacrament is "the holy of holies" (*The Gospel of Philip* 69:24–25), and it ranks above the other sacraments. Its object is to anticipate the final union, which takes place at death.[301]

The Gnostics treasured those incidents in the Gospels which described the close relationship of Christ with women in his circle, especially Mary Magdalene. Through the chaste kiss of fellowship the firmest links in the human chain are formed, for "it is by a kiss that the perfect conceive and give birth." (*The Gospel of Philip* 59:2–3)

Sexual desire is most intense when it is denied fulfilment, and the chaste kiss of the Gnostics continues during the Middle Ages in the *cortezia* of the troubadours, for whom the consummation of the sexual drive was likewise prohibited. It is during this period that sexuality appears most clearly as a symbol for mystical union.[302]

---

299. R. M. Brown and D. A. Bennett, "Magnus Eisengrim" in Sugg, *Jungian Literary Criticism,* 297.

300. *The Gospel of Philip* 68:22–26.

301. Rudolph, *Gnosis,* 245–47.

302. de Rougemont, *Love in the Western World,* 153–59, "Orthodox Mystics and the Language of Passion."

"DREAMING THE MYTH ONWARDS"

THE GNOSTIC CREATION myth probably originated in Jewish speculation on the first chapters of Genesis—speculation that flowed naturally from the parent faith into Christianity. Since the Genesis story of creation has incorporated folkloric material about the loss of innocence through the acquisition of knowledge (cf. Gen. 3:7), it provided a springboard for speculation about the causes of the human predicament and the knowledge of one's true origin in which alone salvation and liberation are to be found.

Gnostic interpretation of Genesis is bizarre and even perverse, from a modern exegetical standpoint. It gives free rein to the inner promptings of the imagination which, in a pre-psychological age, find expression in accounts of the origin of the cosmos. The inner expresses itself in terms of the outer. This apparently arbitrary type of reading finds a surprising defence in a modern literary critic:

> It has been axiomatic in literary criticism that close reading precedes a valid judgment. But in my experience of the literary journals, a close reading often takes one, step by tedious step, away from where one instinctively knows the real value of the work hides. . . . [I]f the life of a book is in its imagery, we will want to keep the images with us, as themselves, for as long as their power moves us.[303]

Creative writing (and reading) is not harnessed to the ego, and the Gnostic reading of Genesis illustrates the problem which James Hillman has been debating: how to get meaning from imagery without converting it into concept.[304] Like a dream, an imaginative text such as Genesis "can only be interpretively re-imagined. . . ."[305]

> Even the best attempts at explanation are only more or less successful translations into another metaphorical language. . . .
> The most we can do is *to dream the myth onwards*. . . .[306]

303. Ralph Maud, "Archetypal Depth Criticism and Melville" in Sugg, *Jungian Literary Criticism*, 260–61.
304. Ibid., 262.
305. Ibid.
306. Jung, *CW*, vol. 9, pt. 1, 160.

This is an apt description of what seems to be happening in the various versions of the Gnostic creation myth. This may explain why the "crazy" world to which the Gnostics bear witness still exerts a powerful fascination today, when infatuation with the magic of technology and progress has resulted in a modern version of the counterfeit reality which the Gnostics sought to unmask.

THE GOSPEL OF THOMAS

ALTHOUGH *The Gospel of Thomas* contains no reference to the Gnostic creation myth, it is clearly Gnostic if gnosis is understood as introverted religious knowledge. The importance of such knowledge is explicitly stated in Saying 3: "When you come to know yourselves, then you will become known." Indeed, one of the most striking characteristics of this text is the importance of "the kingdom within," in contrast to the Synoptic tradition, where apocalyptic sayings overshadow the wisdom material.

We do not know what tradition, written or oral, has elicited the interpretation of Jesus' sayings contained in this text. Some scholars believe that *Thomas* is directly dependent upon the Coptic translation of the Synoptics. This source-critical position leads to the judgment that *Thomas* is a gnosticizing distortion of the Synoptic sayings tradition.[307] Other scholars believe that *Thomas* depends on a tradition which is independent of the Synoptics.[308] I prefer to regard *Thomas* and the Synoptics as alternative interpretations of a sayings tradition which has not been preserved in its original form. *Thomas*'s emphasis on "the kingdom within" may give expression to a dimension of Jesus' teaching which the canonical tradition has chosen to de-emphasize.

The imagery contained in many of the sayings in this collection is most bizarre, and one would do well to follow Hillman's advice and work with the image, not always pressing for a meaning, even though, in an esoteric text, the possibility of some cryptic

---

307. Cf. Michael Fieger, *Das Thomasevangelium* (Münster: Aschendorff, 1991).

308. Cf. J. S. Kloppenborg et al., *Q-Thomas Reader* (Sonoma, Calif.: Polebridge Press, 1990).

signification cannot be ruled out. However, the interpretation of the sayings against the assumed background of a Gnostic dogmatic makes them all mean pretty much the same thing: the striking imagery is flattened into doctrinal uniformity.

One saying, however, has a special relevance for biblical empirics: "When you make the two into one . . . then you will enter [the kingdom]." (Saying 22) We have seen the operation of this principle in the use of scripture in *The Gospel of Truth*: the interpretation is interwoven with the allusion, so that no seams are visible. In other words, the duality between text and interpretation has been overcome: "there is not a subject and an object. . . . 'The eye by which I see God is the same eye by which He sees me.'"[309]

If we extend this principle to the experiential level, transcending the duality between text and reader takes on a quasi-sacramental quality: the reader is in the text and the text is in the reader. Islamic commentators on the Qur'an provide a striking example of this phenomenon.[310]

SACRED SOUND

The Second Book of Jeu contains the following "secret names": *zozeze, persomphon chus, eaza zeozaz zozeoz* (chapter 52). These words are used in connection with the soul's ascent to the kingdom of light, and they might therefore indicate an interest in sacred sound, used in meditation, such as the sacred syllable "OM," which typifies the Hindu gods Brahma, Vishnu, and Shiva. Rudolph[311] reproduces an amulet represented in a third-century Greek papyrus, with an inscription consisting of "magical" words and signs. According to the Naasenes, the "three words" which Jesus spoke to Thomas

---

309. Barthes, *Pleasure of the Text,* 16.

310. Todd Lawson, "The Dangers of Reading: Inlibration, Communion, and Transference in Qur'an Commentary." A paper presented to the Oriental Club of Toronto on Feb. 1, 1994.

311. Rudolph, *Gnosis,* 223.

(Saying 13) were *Kaulkau, Saulasau, Zesar.*[312] It is possible, therefore, that the Gnostics appreciated the power of the acoustic image to the point of dissociating it from semantic content. However, the evidence is too slender to substantiate this intriguing possibility.

CONCLUSION

THOSE WHO USE the label "Gnostic" to discredit any movement in the church of which they disapprove[313] are paying a back-handed compliment to the power of an approach to Christian symbols which ought to have vanished centuries ago with the disappearance of the Gnostics and the Cathars.

We are interested in the Nag Hammadi texts because of their free and unfettered reading of scripture, as well as their remarkable anticipation of certain modern insights about the nature of language.

Anyone who presumes to say, "I have the spirit of God" (1 Cor. 7:40), poses a serious challenge to institutional religion. But the Gnostics' use of scripture is not so very different from that of other pneumatics, like Paul and Jesus, who interpret scripture without regard, it would seem, for either "the intention of the [human] author" or "the analogy of faith" (Rom. 12:6).

In this book I have made no attempt to "validate" this way of reading scripture. I have simply pointed out its existence and proposed a psychological theory which might explain it. My suggestion that the Gnostics may bear witness, at the dawn of Christianity, to the practice of "biblical empirics" does not prove anything. It simply provides an interesting parallel. The popularity—and danger—of gnosis may have been that it provided a lyrical approach to Christian symbols at a time when Christianity was becoming increasingly a prose religion.

---

312. Hippolytus, *Refutatio omnium haeresium,* V,viii,5 (cf. Isa. 28:10).
313. Cf. P. J. Lee, *Against the Protestant Gnostics* (New York: Oxford University Press, 1987).

Conclusion

WE FIND OURSELVES in a curious situation regarding the Bible as we approach the end of the second millennium. On the one hand, we have access to more information *about* the Bible than at any previous period in history. On the other hand, there has never been a time when the Bible has had less influence in mainline Protestant churches, which has led one writer to speak of "the strange silence of the Bible in the Church."[314]

In 1526 William Tyndale made the New Testament available to anyone who could read English, an act considered so radical in its implications that Tyndale would pay for it ten years later at the stake. Today the Bible is readily available to anyone who wants a copy, and most people do have one. But many seem not to know what to do with it:

> More often than not the Bible is found buried on the top shelf of the bookcase in the den or covered with dust on the bottom shelf of the coffee table. If it is read at all, it is used as a desperate treatment for insomnia when drugstore medicines fail.[315]

Although Christians may not challenge the doctrine of biblical inspiration, many no longer seem to regard the Bible as a revelatory text, through which God might actually speak to them.

This situation is the result, in part, of the cultural and societal changes with which we dealt in our first chapter. But it is also the result, paradoxically, of that very growth in knowledge *about* the Bible which has accompanied the popular indifference. Twenty-five years after the appearance of Walter Wink's explosive little book,[316]

---

314. James D. Smart, *The Strange Silence of the Bible in the Church* (Philadelphia: Westminster Press, 1970).

315. Stroup, *Promise of Narrative Theology*, 26.

316. Wink, *The Bible in Human Transformation*.

it is high time for us to acknowledge and take to heart the truth of its central thesis: the way the Bible is studied in the modern world is incapable of delivering what people expect from reading the Bible, namely, "that the past becomes alive and illumines our present with new possibilities for personal and social transformation."[317]

It is pointless to fault historical criticism for not doing what it was never intended to do in the first place. Nevertheless, as long as historical criticism remains "the only game in town," the hope that the Bible can function as an illuminative, transformative, and revelatory text will continue to fade. Indeed, this hope may come to be regarded even by Christians as naive and illusory. For all practical purposes, the Bible will have ceased to function as sacred scripture.

The authors of *The Postmodern Bible* have succinctly expressed the dilemma in which we find ourselves:

> the dominant methodologies of historical criticism have been both the very foundation of modern biblical interpretation and the major obstacle to making sense of the Bible's ongoing formative influence over culture and society.[318]

How is it possible to skirt the "obstacle" without falling back into the precritical dogmatic reading of the Bible which used to be taken for granted in the church and is still normative in many quarters?

Like Wink, I find suggestions for a way out of this dilemma in the writings of C. G. Jung: "Any sacral action, in whatever form, works like a vessel for receiving the contents of the unconscious."[319] Reading the Bible certainly qualifies as a "sacral action," and the biblical text has the capability of functioning as a mediator between consciousness and the unconscious. However, for Bible reading to be "a vessel" it must first be emptied of our ego-centered agendas and preoccupations. Of course, this goes contrary to the way in

---

317. Ibid., 2.

318. *The Postmodern Bible*, George Aichele et al. (New Haven: Yale University Press, 1995), 1.

319. Jung, *CW*, vol. 11, 350

which the Bible is read in both church and academy, and it is also alien to the temper of modern society. Nevertheless, the contents of the unconscious can only manifest themselves if the reader has surrendered control: in an encounter with the unconscious, as with the Deity, the appropriate mental attitude is "Thy will, not mine, be done" (Mark 14:36). The ego can only get in the way, since "[t]he numinous image is far more an expression of essentially unconscious processes than a product of rational inference."[320] Therefore, instead of a reading where the ego calls the shots, I am proposing that we let the Bible "happen" to the ego, in such a way that the Bible becomes an inner therapist, which analyzes the ego's conscious attitude.[321]

Surrendering control is not only difficult but also dangerous. People are afraid that it may lead to going *out* of control, and the dreadful things which have been done in the name of the Bible fully justify this fear; it is indeed a "horrible" book. In a previous chapter, I suggested that abandoning the notion of "legitimacy" in interpretation does not mean surrendering ethical responsibility for the consequences of interpretation. The reader of the Bible cannot claim the privilege enjoyed by the Bible's divine author of being beyond good and evil. By the same token, giving up control when we read the Bible does not entail giving up our responsibility to discern what comes out of the exercise, and to use it in an ethical way.

There is, of course, no guarantee that *anything* will come out of reading the Bible in this manner; biblical empirics is a matter of divine grace, not human effort. Jung observes:

> Experiences cannot be *made*. They happen—yet fortunately their independence of man's activity is not absolute but relative. We can draw closer to them—that much lies within our human reach. . . . The way to experience, moreover, is anything but a clever trick; it is rather a venture which requires us to commit ourselves with our whole being.[322]

---

320. Ibid., 312.
321. Kugler, *Alchemy of Discourse*, 111.
322. Jung, *CW*, vol. 11, 331–32.

The good news is that although the scriptures have been "inter-preted, explained, and dogmatized until they become so encrusted with man-made images that they can no longer be seen,"[323] we continue, nevertheless, to be affected by the Bible in ways which change our lives for the better. But for this to happen, we must be prepared to "shift gears," to move from the head to the heart, that center of the emotions referred to by the Emmaus disciples and by John Wesley. For it is usually when the emotions are brought into play that religious insight emerges.

In our postmodern—and post-Christian—situation, "searching the scriptures" (John 5:39) may lead less frequently than in the past to a realization of some ethical or doctrinal imperative. The insight to which the experience of reading the Bible leads us today may be less clear-cut than some of the examples which we have given: the Emmaus disciples' realization that the Christ must suffer to enter into his glory (Luke 24:26); Antony's decision to dispose of his worldly goods; Augustine's decision to put away his concubine; Luther's sudden realization that faith alone justi-fies, apart from works. But wherever there has been a genuine encounter with God, such as we believe is still possible through reading the scriptural text, the result will be a growth in self-knowledge, and Christians, from Clement of Alexandria to Calvin, have affirmed that whoever knows oneself knows God.

Once we have accepted the words of scripture as "testimonies of the soul" (Tertullian), then history and doctrine, which had both been problematical paradigms for "the truth of the Bible," can take on new meaning and relevance. These last years of the second millennium reveal a curiously ambivalent attitude towards history. On the one hand, we equate "historical" and "true," so that whatever is held to be true on religious grounds *must* be historical, and whatever is deemed unhistorical *cannot* be true. On the other hand, we are also affected by the attitude expressed in Henry Ford's statement that "history is bunk": one need not know the history of the automobile in order to be able to manufacture an automobile. In our society, "instant culture" is the prevailing phenomenon, and our sense of history and tradi-tion is under severe threat.

323. Ibid., 320.

Jung regarded this situation as completely abnormal. He himself had a strong sense of history, both as a person and as a thinker. He was very conscious of his own personal and cultural roots and was always aware of the way in which his own thinking had evolved from that of his predecessors. He believed that the development of the psyche can only be understood in the context of its personal and collective past.[324] In each of us "is written the history of mankind,"[325] and self-knowledge is only possible if we understand the past from which we spring.

To be sure, such an understanding of history as the matrix of human existence is quite different from the [re]constructive hypotheses of the "historical" critic, about which Jung entertained a healthy skepticism. But Jung's understanding is arguably closer to what we mean when we say that Christianity is a "historical" religion than is the "history" which critical research seeks to uncover, for in such research unexpressed and unexamined assumptions— not to mention personal ego—often play a negative role.

Doctrine too takes on new meaning when we understand its relation to the psyche. Jung was deeply concerned about the separation of Western religion from contemporary experience, and his psychological approach to doctrine has given fresh relevance to ideas and practices that many had dismissed as "sacrosanct unintelligibility."[326]

A Psychological Approach to the Dogma of the Trinity begins with a quote from Augustine,[327] and it stands fully in the tradition of *De Trinitate. Transformation Symbolism in the Mass*[328] relates the transubstantiation of bread and wine to the process of human transformation which Jung called "individuation."

> The life of Christ, understood psychologically, represents the vicissitudes of the Self as it undergoes incarnation in an individual ego and of the ego as it participates in that divine drama.[329]

---

324. J. J. Clarke, *In Search of Jung* (London: Routledge, 1992), 48.
325. Jung, *CW,* vol. 6, 338.
326. Ibid., vol. 11, 109.
327. Ibid., 107.
328. Ibid., 201–96.
329. E. F. Edinger, *The Christian Archetype* (Toronto: Inner City Books, 1987), 15.

Incarnation and deification constitute a single process, for only the individual is the bearer of consciousness, and only through the individual's coming to consciousness ("individuation") can God enter this world.

Jung hailed the proclamation of Mary's assumption into heaven as "the most important religious event since the Reformation,"[330] since, for the first time within orthodox Christianity, the feminine was brought into the proximity of the Godhead.

To those who criticize Jung's approach to doctrine as "psychological reductionism" he replies:

> To treat a metaphysical statement as a psychic process is not to say that it is "merely psychic," as my critics assert—in the fond belief that the word "psychic" postulates something known. It does not seem to have occurred to people that when we say "psyche" we are alluding to the densest darkness it is possible to imagine.[331]

But, finally, it is not Jung's treatment of particular doctrines but his understanding of revelation itself which may prove most helpful. In his writings the term is not restricted to past events of salvation history but includes the process of divine self-disclosure within the human soul. Paul's experience on the road to Damascus serves as the prototype for this understanding of revelation:

> True though it may be that this Christ of St. Paul's would hardly have been possible without the historical Jesus, the apparition of Christ came to St. Paul not from the historical Jesus but from the depths of his own unconscious.[332]

The revelation (Gal. 1:16) which Paul received on the Damascus road (cf. Gal. 1:17) can also be mediated by reading scripture. The purpose of this book has been to reaffirm the revelatory function of holy writ.

---

330. Jung, *CW*, vol. 11, 464.
331. Ibid., 296.
332. Ibid., vol. 9, pt. 1, 121.

ALSO PUBLISHED BY CONTINUUM

Paul Q. Beeching
AWKWARD REVERENCE
Reading the New Testament Today

"Beeching has produced an ably organized, well-written, academically competent, and accessible book thoroughly attentive to basic issues."
—*The Living Church*

Harold Bloom
KABBALAH AND CRITICISM

"The essay on Gershom Scholem is in some ways the most lucid thing Bloom has written. Bloomian 'misreading' is indeed creative interpreting, and this book is an excellent introduction."
—John Hollander in *The New Republic*

Stevan L. Davies
JESUS THE HEALER
Possession, Trance, and the Origins of Christianity

"A *tour de force* that opens a whole new vista on Jesus and his followers."
—Walter Wink

David L. Miller, Editor
JUNG AND THE INTERPRETATION
OF THE BIBLE

Includes contributions by Schuyler Brown, D. Andrew Kille, David L. Miller, Michael Willett Newheart, Wayne G. Rollins, and Trevor Watt

---

Jeffrey L. Staley
READING WITH A PASSION
Rhetoric, Autobiography, and the American West in the Gospel of John

"Staley writes with originality as he draws the reader into a fascinating intellectual and spiritual journey."
—*Christianity and Literature*

Murray Stein
PRACTICING WHOLENESS
Analytical Psychology and Jungian Thought

Argues that we need to practice wholeness and engage in the endeavor intentionally. It is a daily activity, one performed to deepen our lives and broaden our expression.
